The Complete

Instant Pot Diabetic Cookbook

Healthy and Delicious Instant Pot Meals with 4-Week Meal Plan for You to Manage Diabetes

By Alice Jenkins

Table of Content

Introduction

Are you suffering from diabetes or any of the related variances?

Do you have a friend or family member suffering from the disease?

Do you own an Instant Pot or do you intend to acquire one to use in the preparation of your meals?

Do you look forward to healthy and delicious foods that will help in fighting diabetes?

The above questions are just a teaser. If you answered a 'YES' to any of the above questions, this book targets you. Yes! It is the best guide for you!

Once a doctor diagnoses you with diabetes, life becomes tough. You realize that the world has turned upside down. Out of nowhere, you are forced to make some pertinent changes to your lifestyle. You need the zeal to adjust and adapt. Many things considered minor become such enormous challenges.

To be able to face the disease and lead a normal healthy life, you need to adapt to one core principal: diet. Before being diagnosed with diabetes, there is a likelihood that the diet was not a significant consideration for you. You followed a healthy diet and ate food without worrying.

With the onset of diabetes, you now realize that any bite you ingest counts. You have to watch out what you eat. You have to do away with most of your favorite treats and avoid the regular staples. Surprisingly, some people realize that insulin is making them add more weight. Furthermore, some dietary measures will result in losing too much weight than required.

This book has been compiled together to ensure you get simple and delicious meals you will enjoy daily. The recipes are healthy and easy to prepare with the usc of the instant pot.

If you live off the recipes in this book, you will manage your diabetes better. Furthermore, you might find that some of your symptoms diminish.

Read on and learn more!

Chapter 1: The Diabetes 101

What is Diabetes?

You will not get an exact definition of the word "diabetes" because there is more than one type. For example, there is Diabetes Insipidus, a condition characterized by heightened thirst and dilute urine. Pre-diabetes is a condition where your sugar level tends to be higher than usual after fasting - the medical term is impaired fasting glucose. The sugar level can also be higher after eating - the medical term is impaired glucose tolerance. Gestational diabetes refers to the type that can occur during pregnancy.

However, when most people say "diabetes", they are likely to be referring to Diabetes Mellitus, which is the condition typified by a high blood sugar level. It is a metabolic condition. The body does not produce the correct level of insulin, or expresses inappropriate response to the produced insulin, and causes the level of glucose in the blood to increase.

The Importance of Insulin

The one common factor, in every type of diabetes, is the function of the hormone, insulin. It is responsible for how your body stores and uses the glucose obtained from the carbohydrates you eat.

The pancreas produces insulin, in what are called beta cells. These cells primary function is to store and release insulin into the bloodstream. The beta cells respond to an increase in the amount of glucose in the blood by secreting insulin.

Glucose is needed by the body, as it is can easily break it down for energy use. A person with low levels of glucose in their bloodstream may feel lethargic, dizzy, and their muscles may shake. However, a person with high amounts of glucose in their blood may experience blurred vision, a frequent urge to urinate, severe thirst, anxiety, muscle tingling, and fatigue.

Having an abnormally low or high level of glucose in your bloodstream is dangerous. Having a low amount of glucose may cause your body and brain to shut down; while too much glucose may be toxic.

A healthy body produces insulin to ensure there is just enough glucose in the bloodstream for it to function on any given day. The amount a person requires varies according to their daily physical activity. An athlete or a person that exercises regularly may need more glucose. A person who is not as active will need less glucose.

How Does Insulin Control Your Blood Sugar?

Understanding how insulin affects your blood sugar level will enable you to understand the different types of Diabetes mellitus. Insulin works to control the glucose in the body in the following way:

1. When a person eats something, it is digested by their stomach and subsequently passes through the small intestine. Here, it is broken down by enzymes into small sugar units, one of which is glucose.

2. The glucose is absorbed by the blood vessels in the small intestine. It then travels to the cells, or parts of the body that need it, such as the brain or muscle tissue. However, the body does not use all the glucose obtained from food. It also stores some of the glucose in various parts of the body, i.e. the liver, fat and muscle cells. This is especially the case if a person is not physically active, or there is a restriction to their activity in some way, e.g. illness.

3. The body releases insulin to control the amount of glucose stored in these cells. This process happens, when blood passes through the pancreas. The pancreas releases the beta cells. If the cells realize there is too much glucose circulating in the body, it will release a proportionate amount of insulin. Insulin then converts the glucose into a form that can be stored. It will not release insulin if the amount of glucose is low.

Without insulin, the human body cannot use glucose or store it for energy. Therefore, glucose will stay in the bloodstream, causing harmful side effects.

The Symptoms and Negatives of Diabetes

Although it may feel as though diabetes on its own is bad enough, the effects of being diabetic can carry on beyond just the superficial things you notice at first. Being diabetic means continually trying to balance your blood sugar. When there are too high or too low levels of blood sugar, this affects your whole body.

> ### *Cardiovascular Disease.*

Your heart and blood vessels are especially vulnerable to blood sugar spikes, and this increases your risk of most cardiovascular problems.

> ### *Nerve Damage.*

High blood sugar can burn or kill the tiny blood vessels that lead to your nerves. Such an action can lead to phantom pain, numbness, digestive problems like nausea or constipation, and even erectile dysfunction.

> ### *Kidney Damage.*

Because your kidneys do the job of filtering out the excess sugar in your blood, if you have a lot of sugar passing through them, you can damage these delicate organs. Severe destruction may result in kidney failure or end-stage kidney disease; which could require dialysis or a transplant.

> ### *Hand and Foot Damage.*

As your nerves and blood vessels die, sometimes tissue in your hands and feet can develop infections and begin to rot.

> ### *Eye Damage.*

If the blood vessels and nerves in your eyes are affected, you can experience partial or complete blindness, or develop cataracts or glaucoma.

> ### *Skin Infections.*

As with hand and foot damage, any cuts to your skin heal poorly and rot, causing infections and sores.

> ### *Urine Infections.*

The sugar in your urine makes you more vulnerable to UTIs.

> ### *Alzheimer's Disease.*

Sometimes called Type-3 Diabetes, Alzheimer's is much more common in people who have diabetes or poor blood sugar control.

> ### *Birth Defects and Stillbirth.*

Pregnant women who have diabetes have high chances of giving birth to huge babies, babies with low blood sugar or have a stillbirth.

> ### *Preeclampsia.*

Preeclampsia is more common in women with diabetes and can be life-threatening to both mother and baby.

> **There are different types of diabetes, as will be discussed below.**

Type-1 Diabetes

This is a chronic condition where the pancreas produces either less or no insulin, though this hormone is to allow sugar or glucose into the cells to produce more energy.

Several aspects can contribute to Diabetes type 1. They include factors like genetics or sometimes viruses.

The early appearances come in the childhood stages or sometimes during the adolescent period; to some extent, it may develop in the adults.

This type is deemed to be very dangerous. It can only be well managed to reduce the blood sugar levels with insulin by carefully checking on the kind of diet as far as lifestyle is concerned. The move aims at reducing the chances of more complications related to it as it is thought to have no permanent cure.

➢ *Symptoms of Type 1.*

Type 1 has its symptoms appear suddenly, and they include the following character traits:

1. There are increased chances that a person is always thirst, and the rate of water consumption is not standard as recommended by the nutritionists.

2. When there is too much drinking of water beyond the recommended volume then, the chances are that there shall be frequent visits to the lavatory. It will then lead us to another sign frequency in urine discharge.

3. When children who never wet their beds during nights start wetting their beds during the night hours, then this becomes a clear indication of this type 1 of diabetes.

4. The time and rate of feeding are at a shorter interval is a likely hood or a clear indication of diabetes. One is always in a hunger state hence feeding all the time.

5. With increased or an intended weight loss in a person without a gym or any stressing factor or other ailment is a clear indication of diabetes.

6. Any unexplained state of one's irritation on situations easily explained is also a measure of diabetes.

7. General body weakness, inability to perform simple chores and general body fatigue becomes another clear indication also.

8. Some people can encounter a blurred vision. It can be an indication of diabetes.

Note: If you note any of the signs in your kids, visit a doctor for a proper direction and prescriptions.

➢ *Causes of Diabetes Type 1.*

The body's immune system is understood to be fighting this dangerous and harmful bacteria and virus. The action mistakenly destroys the insulin-producing (islets, also called islets of Langerhans) that are cells in the pancreas, though some other possible causes include the following as stated below:

1. Family traits from one generation to another can cause Type 1. Hence, one can have it just because one person in his family lineage was with the same condition.

2. The level at which one is exposed to viruses and the different environmental factors may also cause diabetes.

➢ *Remedies of Diabetes Type 1.*

This condition needs to be carefully scrutinized to control more complications as this type is irreversible as its cure has not received full approvals yet. Those involved are advised to seek early clinical trials and carefully weigh the risks and benefits of any treatment available.

Type-2 Diabetes

Here, the body loses the capability to metabolize glucose. It can occur due to ineffectiveness to use produced insulin or is unable to produce insulin. It results in high levels of glucose in the blood that may cause severe damage to body organs. Type 2 diabetes has become very common and found in children, teens, and young adults.

Symptoms: Obesity, eating unhealthy and junk food, having a family history of type 2 diabetes, high blood pressure, high cholesterol level, smoking, lack of physical activity

Compare to type 1 diabetes, type 2 diabetes is a severe condition, and it requires the use of insulin and anti-diabetic injection to keep glucose level under control. Another simple and easy way to reverse type 2 diabetes is regular exercise and eating healthy low-carb and very low-calorie food.

➢ *Type 2 Diabetes vs Type 1 Diabetes*

Remember how insulin helps break down glucose into energy, i.e. that is what occurs in non-diabetics. In Type 1, the body produces significantly less or no insulin that is needed by the body. However, in type 2 diabetes, this is what happens:

- Glucose passes through the pancreas and triggers the beta cells to produce insulin.

- The body does not have a problem producing insulin. The insulin carries out its role and directs glucose to the cells, including fat and muscle cells.

- However, in type 2 diabetes, the cells resist the insulin and refuse to accept the glucose. Alternatively, there is an agent present in the cell, which refuses to recognize the insulin, keeping it and the glucose out of the cell. The glucose does not go directly to the cells.

- Glucose is pushed back into the bloodstream and remains there, until external intervention, e.g. medication.

In type 1 diabetes, the cell does not absorb the glucose; therefore, the organs are unable to function due to a lack of fuel. In type 2 diabetes, some glucose may still make it inside the cells, although the energy acquired may not be enough to make the organ function correctly.

➢ **Causes of Type 2 Diabetes**

The cause for type 2 diabetes is lifestyle and genetics. The following may increase a person's risk of acquiring type 2 diabetes: or

- Consuming a lot of carbohydrates and simple sugars

- Low physical activity, or a sedentary lifestyle

- Being overweight or obese

- Hormonal imbalance - that results in an abnormal increase in appetite

- Having direct relatives with a history of diabetes, e.g. Mother or Father

Gestational Diabetes

Gestational diabetes is the result of high glucose levels during pregnancy. It usually develops in the third trimester and disappears when the baby born. Gestational diabetes occurs due to hormonal changes in the second or third trimester. As the baby grows, the need for insulin also increases by two to three times. But if the body fails to produce enough insulin, a simple sugar (glucose) won't move into the cells and stays in the blood. This causes high sugar levels and leads to gestational diabetes.

Finding out that you have gestational diabetes during one of the happiest times of life is indeed overwhelming. And, you may think it's too late to find out diabetes. But you can still get treatment. After making healthy changes in your life, you can lead a healthy and happy pregnancy without causing any harm to your body and baby.

➢ *Cause of Gestational Diabetes and Who Are at Risk*

When a woman is pregnant, she needs a higher dose of insulin because she must provide glucose to the unborn baby. Her own body may become insulin resistant due to hormonal imbalance during pregnancy.

In typical situations, the baby resolves this as it receives the excess glucose. However, if the baby is also insulin resistant, it will not receive enough glucose for its needs. The excess glucose the baby cannot absorb returns to the mother, causing her blood glucose levels to rise.

Women with the following characteristics have a higher risk of developing gestational diabetes:

1. Between the age of twenty-five and forty-five years old

2. A normal weight before pregnancy

3. Parents that have a history of diabetes

4. Did not eat an excess of sugary food, prior to pregnancy

5. Previously gave birth to a baby weighing more than eight pounds

6. If they were born with the disorder, macrosomia.

> *Those Who Are Between Twenty-Five To Forty-Five Years Old*

A woman *under thirty years* of age, but *over twenty-five*, has a higher chance of her diabetes being gestational diabetes unless a problem with her pancreas is discovered.

Type 1 diabetic patients are normally diagnosed before the age of twenty. So, unless the pregnant woman has developed a disease in her pancreas, there is no reason she would produce less or no amount of insulin.

Type 2 diabetic patients experience symptoms at age thirty and over. So, if the pregnant woman is below that age, her diabetes may only be gestational diabetes.

However, some pregnant women develop high blood sugar when they are over thirty years. Such diabetes will not be declared gestational unless a proper investigation happens.

> *A Normal Weight Before Pregnancy*

Pregnancy can cause sudden hormonal imbalances in women. The hormones may trigger an increase in appetite and weight gain, which could even be borderline obesity. The body automatically defends itself from this sudden imbalance by making the cells resistant to insulin.

> *Parents That Have a History Of Diabetes*

Diabetes is hereditary. A person who has at least one diabetic parent has a higher risk of acquiring the disease. If the pregnant woman is over thirty years old and her parent or parents have diabetes, she should be investigated thoroughly, before ruling out chronic diabetes.

If she is below thirty and one or both of her parents have a history of diabetes, there is a higher chance the diabetes is temporary.

A pregnant woman is at a higher risk of having type 2 diabetes, once she is older than thirty years old.

> *Does Not Eat An Excess Of Sugary Food, Prior To Pregnancy*

Type 2 diabetes develops because of high carbohydrate or high sugar diet. If a pregnant woman has been observing this type of diet before pregnancy and has high glucose amounts in her blood; she may not have gestational diabetes. She may have type 2 diabetes. This is more likely if she is age thirty or older

> *Previously Gave Birth To a Baby Weighing More Than Eight Pounds*

Women who previously gave birth to young ones weighing eight pounds or more have a higher risk of developing gestational diabetes. Not unless the genetics of the parents offsets the size of the baby.

Studies show that as a baby receives the same nutrients as the mother, it also acquires the high glucose level in the mother's blood, while in the womb. The increase in the glucose level may cause them to grow abnormally.

> *An Individual Born With Macrosomia.*

Women who are born with the condition - macrosomia (i.e. she weighed more than eight pounds when born), are prone to gestational diabetes and type 2 diabetes.

The Relationship Between Food and Type-2 Diabetes

Eating healthy meals and doing a physical activity not only control the effect of diabetes, but they can also create a positive impact on overall health. To manage the effects of diabetes, you need to balance what you drink and eat with being active and taking diabetic medicines. The levels of glucose can be kept in check with the types of food you eat, the amounts and the time of eating.

Indeed, making changes in your eating and drinking habits is challenging in the beginning. Once your body gets habitual with your new lifestyle, you can achieve your health goal in no time.

So being a person with diabetes doesn't mean that eating those foods that you don't enjoy. Not at all. You have the freedom to eat everything you love, but you have to consume small portions and less often. You can do this with the plate method. This method adds a variety of food in your plate and helps you control your portion sizes. For example, you can divide a plate into three portions, half of the plate for non-starchy veggies, the one-fourth portion for protein and the other one-fourth portion for grains, along with some fruits and a glass of low-fat milk.

The Diet Changes

Diabetes *cannot* be cured with diet alone. Many health gurus and nutritionists will tell you they can cure your diabetes because they want to sell you a book, or a three-week course. The reality is that many factors come together to cause diabetes, and diet is only one of them.

If you want to reverse your diabetes, first of all, you need to know if it is reversible. Start by finding out whether you caused your diabetes, or whether it happened on its own. If your diabetes developed due to things beyond your control, you might not be able to reverse it.

A healthy diet is good in managing your diabetes, but you will need other things as well. Exercise, medication, supplements, or even surgery may be required to make you healthier. Talk to your doctor, or, ideally, a specialist, about what it would take to reverse your type of diabetes.

Remember, doing all the right things does not mean your diabetes will magically go away. Maybe there were many factors, one of them being genetic, and you cannot get rid of your diabetes. Maybe you can be symptom-free for a long time, but relapse every time you eat high-risk foods. Or maybe you can reverse your diabetes, but some of the complications, such as heart or kidney problems, do not go away.

Any improvement, however small, is for the better. It is a fact that you cannot cure your diabetes. Just making your everyday life easier and your health a bit better is worth its weight in gold.

> *Nutritional Balance*

What makes a good diet for a person with diabetes?

It does not depend on the diabetes variant you are suffering. Your medication, exercise, or long term healthcare plans do not matter a lot. Your ideal diet is going to be quite similar to any other diabetic's diet. Starting with nutritional balance, you need to make sure you are eating the right ratio of fat, protein, and carbohydrate. You also need to make sure you are eating the right types of carbohydrate, as there are vast differences between carbohydrates, the healthy and unhealthy varieties.

Your carbohydrate needs are no different as a person with diabetes than they were before diabetes. You still need, at most, 50% of your calories from carbohydrates, which equals 300g. However, if you are used to eating less, try and eat less. Fats are not as harmful as we have been made to believe, and a diet with healthy fats is no problem. Just be careful if your gallbladder is affected, and avoid trans fats. Remember, protein can be broken down into glucose. So if you ingest a meal containing high amounts of proteins, you must check your blood sugar one or two hours after eating. m

Finally, you need to consider what micronutrients you are getting and what ones you need. Our micronutrients come in four types: vitamins, minerals, antioxidants, and fiber. Make sure to eat a balanced amount of all the necessary vitamins and minerals. Pay special attention to Vitamin D; it regulates hormones and helps you make insulin, and chromium, which lowers your blood sugar levels.

When it comes to antioxidants, consider a trans-resveratrol supplement to help your body heal and reduce inflammation. Another suggestion concerns fiber; make sure to eat the recommended amount, and ideally twice the recommended amount. It slows down digestion; preventing blood sugar spikes and hunger.

Principles of The Diabetic Diet

Experts say that the ideal diabetic diet has the following characteristics:

1. It Is Low In Calories

People with diabetes should eat a low-calorie diet, as opposed to a low carbohydrate diet, especially type 2 diabetics. Lowering calories means you lower the actual amount of carbohydrate and fat you need to burn.

Low-carbohydrate and low-fat diets may not work for people with diabetes, as they may then increase proteins in the digestive tract and the bloodstream to a dangerous level. Diabetic people, especially those with type 2 diabetes, should not consume a large amount of protein, as it may increase their risk of neuropathy and other complications. If the amount of fat and carbs, in the diet, is significantly decreased, while the amount of protein remains at a proportionate level, the diabetic may suffer from malnutrition. Thus, the solution is to lower the overall calorie intake.

2. The Number of Carbohydrates Should Not Be Less Than 45%, But No More Than 60% Of The Total Calorie Intake Each Day.

These levels of carbohydrates (45% to 60%) are considered the safe amount for a diabetic to consume.

If a diabetic observes an 1800-calorie daily allowance, the number of carbohydrates he/she eats should be within 810 to 1080 calories.

For pregnant and breastfeeding women, the amount should not be less than 50%.

3. The Amount of Protein Should Not Exceed 1 Gram, For Every 0.45kg Of His/Her Ideal Weight, And No Lower Than 0.4 Grams.

Diabetic patients, especially those with type 2 diabetes, should not consume too much protein. It may worsen their nephropathy and make them more prone to dehydration.

Previously, nutritionists suggested the protein intake of diabetic patients should be 15 to 20% of their total calorie intake for the day. However, the amount of protein should be proportionate to the weight of the person.

4. The Amount of Fat In a Diabetic's Diet Should Not Be More Than 25% Of The Amount Of The Ideal Total Calorie Allowance For The Day.

Some dieters often allocate the remaining amount of the "ideal total calories" each day to fat. So, if the remaining amount is 35%, that would be the amount of fat in their diet.

Many experts disagree. The percentage of fat should be low, especially if the person is over twenty-five years old. Too much fat, whether from a good source or not, can still lead to complications, such as heart disease and hypertension. Also, it interferes with insulin receptors, causing glucose levels to rise.

5. Their Diet Should Have Less Fried And Processed Food.

Fried and processed foods are high in unhealthy fat and refined carbohydrates. They increase the level of glucose in the blood, blocking insulin receptors and increasing cravings for sweet and greasy food.

Foods that retain their natural flavor are usually high in fiber and low in sugar. Fiber aids digestion and helps "choose" which nutrients are absorbed, or not, by the body.

Foods to Choose

When you have diabetes, it can feel as though there is nothing you can eat anymore. Rest assured there are plenty of perfectly safe foods if you know where to look. There are plenty of foods that will improve your symptoms and make your life easier.

- ✓ Whole grains.
- ✓ Low carb tubers and roots.
- ✓ The fresh, frozen, or raw vegetables.
- ✓ Fresh fruit with high fiber content.
- ✓ Fresh berries with low sugar content.
- ✓ Non-sweet fruits.
- ✓ Sugar-free and calorie-free products.
- ✓ Freshly boiled beans. Tinned and refried beans are higher in simple carbs.
- ✓ Nuts and seeds - dry roasted or raw; walnuts, almonds, pistachios, and peanuts.
- ✓ Fresh meat.
- ✓ Whole dairy.
- ✓ Black coffee.

Foods to Avoid

All that said, there is a host of foods you really should not be eating when you have diabetes. Some of these are common knowledge. But there are others which everyone seems to assume are suitable for those who have diabetes for being low in carbs, high in protein, or high in fiber. They are so high on the glycemic index (GI); they are dangerous.

- White grains. Includes "whole wheat" and "whole meal." If it is not "whole grain," it is out.

- Potatoes. Sweet potatoes are safe, but their GI is very high.

- Breakfast cereals.

- Sweet and squishy fruits. Avoid fruits like bananas, mangoes, or melons that are high in sugar and not as high in fiber as other fruits.

- Canned fruits. They are always preserved in syrup or juice.

- Jelly and jam. Choose ones specially formulated for diabetics.

- Breadcrumbs.

- Deep-fried foods.

- Gravies and sauces.

- Low-fat dairy (sweetened).

- Sugary drinks.

- Beer.

- Fruit juice.

- Smoothies.

- Flavored hot drinks.

Lifestyle Changes To Fight Diabetes

Treatment of Diabetes varies from patient to patient depending on the type of Diabetes one has. For those with type 1 diabetes insulin pump is an alternative to inject with an insulin pen since it's more flexible to manage diabetes with proper guidelines. Besides, one can opt for islet cell transplant as it stops one from experiencing severe hypos

Furthermore, type 2 diabetes patients may need tablets, i.e., metformin. They stimulate the pancreas to produce insulin though it's advisable to seek assistance from the doctor on the best tablets for your medication. However, weight loss surgery for stomach and intestines helps you lose weight.

It is vital for people with diabetes to be physically active. Insulin resistance goes down when you exercise, enabling the body to use glucose more effectively and avoid long time complications like heart problems. Exercise also maintains good cholesterol, improves body sensitivity to insulin and delays or prevent diabetes. Diabetic patients have the understanding that the ailment can be controlled since the hemoglobin tests are conducted, which shows levels of blood glucose for the past months. For the non- diabetic people, the level goes below 5%.

However, the complication of diabetes can be prevented by:

- Staying physically active.
- Going for regular eye check-ups.
- Taking medicine regularly.
- Being aware of skin infections.
- Maintaining a healthy diet.
- Taking special care of the feet by watching out for any wounds or loss of sensation.

In the same way, diabetes be prevented and controlled by;

- Through exercise and a good diet.
- Avoiding the use of alcohol and tobacco.
- Going for regular test on blood glucose.
- Maintaining a healthy body weight.
- Stress management.

Chapter 2: The Instant Pot Basics

The instant pot is the fastest-growing kitchen appliance in the culinary market. This multi-purpose pressure cooker has automated conventional pressure cooking and promotes hassle-free cooking. It's a blessing for individuals who despite being busy, prefers home-cooked food and are health conscious. Instant pot simplifies exhaustive cooking. There is no need to stir food frequently, keep a check on cooking temperature, move food from one pan to another, and only one pot to wash. Now, there could not be any excuse not to prepare a home-cooked meal.

To name but a few benefits, instant pot saves time, retain food nutrients, and enhance its texture and taste. Let's check out how instant pot makes cooking so easy and simple.

Top 7 Benefits of Instant Pot

- The instant pot is an advanced machine that does the job of seven. It is a frying/sautéing pan, simmering pot, steamer, warming pot, rice cooker, slow cooker, and a yogurt maker. Yes, it is a jack of all trades, you can cook anything and everything in it.

- With so many built-in functions in the instant pot, one could imagine its operation's super complicated. No! Just dump your food into the inner pot, and press a few buttons and your food is good to go for cooking.

- The instant pot is an energy-efficient cooking appliance. It is evaluated that instant pot reduces energy and cooking time by 70 percent for frying, sautéing, boiling, baking, and steaming of food. It does this by using its inner pot, which is fully insulated. It ensures that an instant pot doesn't exert too much energy for heating. Moreover, instant pot requires only less cooking liquid than other cooking methods, and thus, food is boiled faster in it.

- Boiling tends to diminish nutrients in food. However, boiling in instant pot is so faster and evenly, which allow foods to retain their nutrients.

- Cooking in open utensils expose food to heat and oxygen that diminished flavors and change texture. With the airtight cooking in the instant pot, the food retains its bright color and enable flavor to infuse in each other in record time, and more profoundly.

- Cooking is not something funny and nor pretty. And, on a hot day, cooking is much like working in a hot sauna bathroom. But not anymore! Now, you can walk away from food in instant pot and continue with your work. Moreover, it won't heat its surroundings, so there is no noise, no smell, and no heat while cooking with the instant pot.

- Instant pot can cook for everyone, be it an individual, couple, medium-size family and a crowd. It comes with all sizes, from 2 to 12 quarts, and range of cooking options. And, the best part, it's also not heavy to move around in the kitchen.

Instant Pot Accessories

There are three major parts of an electric pressure cooker – the housing, the inner pot, and the lid.

➢ *The Inner Pot*

It is the removable cooking pot generally made from aluminum, and in higher quality pots, stainless steel. The inner pot is dishwasher safe, and the size usually ranges from 3 to 6 liters or 5.3 to 10.5 pints. It is where you will cook your food in.

➢ *The Lid Lock*

The lid of an Instant Pot has a sealing ring or a gasket. When you close and lock the lid, it will make an airtight chamber, which builds up the pressure inside when the pot is heated. The Instant Pot has a safety design that detects if you did not close the lid properly. When this happens, the pot will not switch on for heating.

➢ *Safety Valves*

The Instant Pot has two safety valves – the float valve with a safety pin and the pressure release regulator valve.

Some models of electric pressure cooker have a safety pin, which prevents a user to accidentally open the pot while there is still significant pressure inside. The safety pin is a float valve that is pushed when pressure is achieved, serving as a latch lock that will prevent the lid from opening under pressure.

The pressure release regulator valve is designed not to release pressure during cooking, and it is where the steam or pressure is released after cooking. In conventional electric pressure cookers, the valve will be pushed up if there is excessive pressure in the pot. In an instant pot, the valve will only release excessive pressure caused by electronic failure.

> ### *The Housing*

It holds the inner pot, and this is where the control box, heating element, and the sensors are located. The control box is the heart and soul of an Instant Pot. The control box is what regulates and monitors temperature and the pressure of the pot when you are cooking. When you press a button, it's what controls the time, the heating, and the cooking cycles.

Understanding instant pot settings and buttons

What ARE all these buttons? Glad you asked! The Instant Pot, depending on your model, has three different types of buttons: pre-set buttons, specific item buttons, and adjusting buttons.

> ### *Pre-Set Buttons.*

These buttons are quite simply normal buttons that are calibrated to cook at a certain pressure or temperature for a certain amount of time. The Instant Pot doesn't know what you've put in; that button is just a safe amount of time for cooking that food type.

MANUAL: Cooks at the highest pressure. Press it and use the + and – buttons to choose your cooking time.

SOUP: High pressure for 20-40 minutes.

MEAT: High pressure for 20-45 minutes.

BEAN: High pressure for 25-40 minutes.

POULTRY: High pressure for 5-30 minutes.

SLOW COOK: No-pressure for a slow cook.

MULTIGRAIN: High pressure for 20-40 minutes.

PORRIDGE: High pressure for 15-30 minutes.

STEAM: High-pressure continuous heat.

> ### *Specific Item Buttons.*

Not all Instant Pots have these, but some have buttons for specific items, such as for boiling eggs, baking bread, or making yogurt. These programs are so specific that they will not cook anything else properly.

SAUTE: Brown food with the lid off.

WARM: Keeps food warm and ready for the table without overcooking it.

RICE: Only white rice.

EGGS: Only eggs.

BREAD: Bread maker function.

YOGURT: Ferments yogurt.

> ### *Adjusting Buttons.*

You don't even need to touch these as a beginner Instant Pot user. They alter the program you have selected or allow you to create your program.

+ AND : Increase or decrease times, pressure, and temperatures.

PRESSURE: Swap between high and low pressure.

ADJUST: Adjust settings.

TIMER: Select a cooking button and time, then hit this button and decide how many minutes the Instant Pot should wait before beginning.

Tips for Cleaning Your Instant Pot

Instant pot requires cleaning do prevent food residues, weird smells due to pressure cooking and clogging. Here are some cleaning steps which every instant pot owner should know.

1. Clean The Main Cooker And Base

When you are ready to clean instant pot, unplug it and make no other contact with an electric source is there.

Take out the inner pot from its base. Then use a clean and damp towel to wipe clean the base, outside and inside of the main cooker. Brush the cooker with a pastry brush or paintbrush to remove all nook and crannies of the cooker and do away with food debris from its bottom. Wipe clean with a dry cloth at the end.

2. Clean The Lid And Its Small Parts

Wash the lid with warm soapy water. Then Remove quick release handle and steam valve and wash them with warm soapy water to remove blocked food residues. Detach the condensation cup and wash it until clean or replace it.

Wash sealing ring in the lid. It prevents absorption of food colors and their odors by the rind. It is recommended to wash the sealing ring in the top rack of the dishwasher. If you notice any crack or deformity in the ring, place the ring immediately.

If the sealing ring has taken any food smell, deodorize it by cleaning with giving it vinegar steam. For this, pour 1 cup water and 1 cup vinegar into the inner pot along with some lemon peels. Shut instant pot with lid and steam for 2 minutes, and do natural pressure release. Open the instant pot, remove the sealing ring, and let dry at room temperature.

3. Scrub The Inner Pot

Wash inner pot in dishwater but make sure it is dishwasher safe.

If there are any stains in the inner pot, soak the instant pot in vinegar for 5 minutes, then rinse it and wash with soapy water. To remove food stains from the inner pot, soak the pot in warm soapy water, then use a damp sponge to scrub away the food residue and rinse the inner pot.

Then use paper towels and vinegar to wipe clean it. Such an action will return the shine of instant pot and remove detergent residues. Then Wipe clean the inside and outside of the inner pot with a wet kitchen cloth.

Wash steamer rack or trivet stand with warm soapy water and wipe clean with paper towels.

4. Wipe The Outside of Instant Pot

Take a damp sponge or kitchen towels and use it to clean the outer body of the instant pot gently. Remove any stains with white vinegar, followed by cleaning with a damp kitchen towel.

5. Reassemble Instant Pot

Finally, set together all the instant pot pieces and reassemble it.

Instant Pot Cooking Timetable For The Diabetic Diet

> ➤ **Dried Beans, Legumes and Lentils**

Dried Beans and Legume	Dry (in Minutes)	Soaked (in Minutes)
Soy beans	25 – 30	20 – 25
Scarlet runner	20 – 25	10 – 15
Pinto beans	25 – 30	20 – 25
Peas	15 – 20	10 – 15
Navy beans	25 – 30	20 – 25
Lima beans	20 – 25	10 – 15
Lentils, split, yellow (moong dal)	15 – 18	N/A
Lentils, plit, red	15 – 18	N/A
Lentils, mini, green (brown)	15 – 20	N/A
Lentils, French green	15 – 20	N/A
Kidney white beans	35 – 40	20 – 25
Kidney red beans	25 – 30	20 – 25
Great Northern beans	25 – 30	20 – 25
Gandules (pigeon peas)	20 – 25	15 – 20
Chickpeas (garbanzo bean chick peas, or kabuli)	35 – 40	20 – 25
Cannellini beans	35 – 40	20 – 25
Black-eyed peas	20 – 25	10 – 15

Black beans	20 – 25	10 – 15
Anasazi	20 – 25	10 – 15
Adzuki	20 – 25	10 – 15

> ➢ **Vegetables (fresh/frozen)**

Vegetable	Fresh (minutes)	Frozen (minutes)
Zucchini, slices or chunks	2 to 3	3 to 4
Yam, whole, small	10 to 12	12 to 14
Yam, whole, large	12 to 15	15 to 19
Yam, in cubes	7 to 9	9 to 11
Turnip, chunks	2 to 4	4 to 6
Tomatoes, whole	3 to 5	5 to 7
Tomatoes, in quarters	2 to 3	4 to 5
Sweet potato, whole, small	10 to 12	12 to 14
Sweet potato, whole, large	12 to 15	15 to 19
Sweet potato, in cubes	7 to 9	9 to 11
Sweet pepper, slices or chunks	1 to 3	2 to 4
Squash, butternut, slices or chunks	8 to 10	10 to 12
Squash, acorn, slices or chunks	6 to 7	8 to 9
Spinach	1 to 2	3 to 4
Rutabaga, slices	3 to 5	4 to 6
Rutabaga, chunks	4 to 6	6 to 8
Pumpkin, small slices or chunks	4 to 5	6 to 7

Pumpkin, large slices or chunks	8 to 10	10 to 14
Potatoes, whole, large	12 to 15	15 to 19
Potatoes, whole, baby	10 to 12	12 to 14
Potatoes, in cubes	7 to 9	9 to 11
Peas, in the pod	1 to 2	2 to 3
Peas, green	1 to 2	2 to 3
Parsnips, sliced	1 to 2	2 to 3
Parsnips, chunks	2 to 4	4 to 6
Onions, sliced	2 to 3	3 to 4
Okra	2 to 3	3 to 4
Mixed vegetables	2 to 3	3 to 4
Leeks	2 to 4	3 to 5
Greens (collards, beet greens, spinach, kale, turnip greens, swiss chard) chopped	3 to 6	4 to 7
Green beans, whole	2 to 3	3 to 4
Escarole, chopped	1 to 2	2 to 3
Endive	1 to 2	2 to 3
Eggplant, chunks or slices	2 to 3	3 to 4
Corn, on the cob	3 to 4	4 to 5
Corn, kernels	1 to 2	2 to 3
Collard	4 to 5	5 to 6
Celery, chunks	2 to 3	3 to 4
Cauliflower flowerets	2 to 3	3 to 4
Carrots, whole or chunked	2 to 3	3 to 4

Carrots, sliced or shredded	1 to 2	2 to 3
Cabbage, red, purple or green, wedges	3 to 4	4 to 5
Cabbage, red, purple or green, shredded	2 to 3	3 to 4
Brussel sprouts, whole	3 to 4	4 to 5
Broccoli, stalks	3 to 4	4 to 5
Broccoli, flowerets	2 to 3	3 to 4
Beets, small roots, whole	11 to 13	13 to 15
Beets, large roots, whole	20 to 25	25 to 30
Beans, green/yellow or wax, whole, trim ends and strings	1 to 2	2 to 3
Asparagus, whole or cut	1 to 2	2 to 3
Artichoke, whole, trimmed without leaves	9 to 11	11 to 13
Artichoke, hearts	4 to 5	5 to 6

➢ **Meat**

Meat and Cuts	Cooking Time (minutes)
Veal, roast	35 to 45
Veal, chops	5 to 8
Turkey, drumsticks (leg)	15 to 20
Turkey, breast, whole, with bones	25 to 30
Turkey, breast, boneless	15 to 20
Quail, whole	8 to 10
Pork, ribs	20 to 25
Pork, loin roast	55 to 60

Pork, butt roast	45 to 50
Pheasant	20 to 25
Lamb, stew meat	10 to 15
Lamb, leg	35 to 45
Lamb, cubes,	10 t0 15
Ham slice	9 to 12
Ham picnic shoulder	25 to 30
Duck, whole	25 to 30
Duck, with bones, cut up	10 to 12
Cornish Hen, whole	10 to 15
Chicken, whole	20 to 25
Chicken, legs, drumsticks, or thighs	10 to 15
Chicken, with bones, cut up	10 to 15
Chicken, breasts	8 to 10
Beef, stew	15 to 20
Beef, shanks	25 to 30
Beef, ribs	25 to 30
Beef, steak, pot roast, round, rump, brisket or blade, small chunks, chuck,	25 to 30
Beef, pot roast, steak, rump, round, chuck, blade or brisket, large	35 to 40
Beef, ox-tail	40 to 50
Beef, meatball	10 to 15
Beef, dressed	20 to 25

> **Fish and Seafood**

Fish and Seafood	Fresh (minutes)	Frozen (minutes)
Shrimp or Prawn	1 to 2	2 to 3
Seafood soup or stock	6 to 7	7 to 9
Mussels	2 to 3	4 to 6
Lobster	3 to 4	4 to 6
Fish, whole (snapper, trout, etc.)	5 to 6	7 to 10
Fish steak	3 to 4	4 to 6
Fish fillet,	2 to 3	3 to 4
Crab	3 to 4	5 to 6

> **Rice and Grains**

Rice & Grain	Water Quantity (Grain : Water ratios)	Cooking Time (in Minutes)
Wheat berries	1:03	25 to 30
Spelt berries	1:03	15 to 20
Sorghum	1:03	20 to 25
Rice, wild	1:03	25 to 30
Rice, white	01:01.5	8
Rice, Jasmine	1:01	4 to 10
Rice, Brown	01:01.3	22 to 28
Rice, Basmati	01:01.5	4 to 8
Quinoa, quick cooking	1:02	8

Porridge, thin	1:6 ~ 1:7	15 to 20
Oats, steel-cut	2/3/2016 1:01	10
Oats, quick cooking	2/3/2016 1:01	6
Millet	2/3/2016 1:01	10 to 12
Kamut, whole	1:03	10 to 12
Couscous	1:02	5 to 8
Corn, dried, half	1:03	25 to 30
Congee, thin	1:6 ~ 1:7	15 to 20
Congee, thick	1:4 ~ 1:5	15 to 20
Barley, pot	1:3 ~ 1:4	25 to 30
Barley, pearl	1:04	25 to 30

➢ **Fruits**

Fruits	Fresh (in Minutes)	Dried (in Minutes)
Raisins	N/A	4 to 5
Prunes	2 to 3	4 to 5
Pears, whole	3 to 4	4 to 6
Pears, slices or halves	2 to 3	4 to 5
Peaches	2 to 3	4 to 5
Apricots, whole or halves	2 to 3	3 to 4
Apples, whole	3 to 4	4 to 6
Apples, in slices or pieces	2 to 3	3 to 4

Chapter 3: 4-Week Meal Plan

Week 1

Day 1

Breakfast: Spicy tofu scramble

Lunch: Wild Rice Salad with Cranberries and Almonds

Dinner: Lamb and chickpea stew

Dessert/Snack/Appetizer: Brussels sprouts

Day 2

Breakfast: Breakfast beans

Lunch: Buffalo chicken chili

Dinner: Beef bourguignon stew

Dessert/Snack/Appetizer: Garlic and herb carrots

Day 3

Breakfast: Cheesy eggs

Lunch: Pumpkin soup

Dinner: Lamb curry

Dessert/Snack/Appetizer: Cilantro lime drumsticks

Day 4

Breakfast: Eggs and bacon

Lunch: Steamed asparagus

Dinner: Shrimp with tomatoes and feta

Dessert/Snack/Appetizer: Eggplant spread

Breakfast: Spicy tofu scramble

Lunch: Asparagus risotto

Dinner: Butter chicken

Dessert/Snack/Appetizer: Cauliflower mash

Breakfast: Eggs and tomato

Lunch: Eggplant curry

Dinner: Rosemary salmon

Dessert/Snack/Appetizer: Pecan pie cheesecake

Breakfast: Breakfast beans

Lunch: Instant Pot Chicken Breast

Dinner: Squash medley

Dessert/Snack/Appetizer: Cheesecake

Week 2

Breakfast: Cheesy eggs

Lunch: Strawberry Farro Salad

Dinner: Lemon pepper and dill salmon

Dessert/Snack/Appetizer: Chocolate cheesecake

Breakfast: Eggs and bacon

Lunch: Tofu curry

Dinner: Coconut shrimp curry

Dessert/Snack/Appetizer: Pumpkin custard

Breakfast: Spicy tofu scramble

Lunch: Vegetable and brown rice stuffed bell peppers

Dinner: Moroccan chicken bowls

Dessert/Snack/Appetizer: Molten brownie cups

Breakfast: Eggs and tomato

Lunch: Lemon chicken with garlic

Dinner: Stuffed sweet potatoes

Dessert/Snack/Appetizer: Cilantro lime drumsticks

Breakfast: Eggs and bacon

Lunch: Lentil and eggplant stew

Dinner: Lamb shoulder

Dessert/Snack/Appetizer: Chocolate cheesecake

Breakfast: Breakfast beans

Lunch: Couscous Tomatoes

Dinner: Pork carnitas

Dessert/Snack/Appetizer: Cauliflower mash

Breakfast: Cheesy eggs

Lunch: Lemon pepper salmon

Dinner: Wild rice pilaf

Dessert/Snack/Appetizer: Cheesecake

Week 3

Breakfast: Sausage breakfast casserole

Lunch: Wheat Berry, Black Bean, and Avocado Salad

Dinner: Beef pot roast

Dessert/Snack/Appetizer: Roasted parsnips

Breakfast: Hazelnut chocolate oats

Lunch: Split pea stew

Dinner: Trout bake

Dessert/Snack/Appetizer: Caramelized carrot and onion

Breakfast: Eggs and mushroom

Lunch: Yellow Lentils

Dinner: Pork Roast

Dessert/Snack/Appetizer: Chili Green Beans

Breakfast: Spanish eggs

Lunch: Cilantro lime chicken

Dinner: Barley Pilaf with Tofu

Dessert/Snack/Appetizer: Mushroom tofu scramble

Breakfast: Berry oats

Lunch: Mussels and spaghetti squash

Dinner: Chicken tikka masala

Dessert/Snack/Appetizer: Carrot hummus

Breakfast: Eggs and mushroom

Lunch: Tomato and cheddar soup

Dinner: Cod in white sauce

Dessert/Snack/Appetizer: Spiced Pear Applesauce

Breakfast: Sausage breakfast casserole

Lunch: Kidney bean stew

Dinner: Chicken piccata

Dessert/Snack/Appetizer: Apple Crunch

Week 4

Breakfast: Hazelnut chocolate oats

Lunch: Chili sin carne

Dinner: Tuna sweetcorn casserole

Dessert/Snack/Appetizer: Goat Cheese–Stuffed Pears

Breakfast: Eggs and mushroom

Lunch: Beef Stroganoff

Dinner: Black Beans, Corn, and Cheese on Sweet Potato

Dessert/Snack/Appetizer: Chai Pear-Fig Compote

Breakfast: Spanish eggs

Lunch: Chick Pea Curry

Dinner: Swordfish steak

Dessert/Snack/Appetizer: Chocolate Chip Banana Cake

Breakfast: Sausage breakfast casserole

Lunch: Chickpea Salad

Dinner: Balsamic Beef Pot Roast

Dessert/Snack/Appetizer: Roasted parsnips

Breakfast: Berry oats

Lunch: Fried tofu hotpot

Dinner: Mustard Pork Chops

Dessert/Snack/Appetizer: Goat Cheese–Stuffed Pears

Breakfast: Hazelnut chocolate oats

Lunch: Black and Pinto Bean Chili

Dinner: Turkey Burger Patty

Dessert/Snack/Appetizer: Chili Green Beans

Breakfast: Spanish eggs

Lunch: Lentil and chickpea curry

Dinner: Spinach Stuffed Chicken Breast

Dessert/Snack/Appetizer: Spiced Pear Applesauce

Chapter 4: The Wonderful Recipes

Breakfast

Spicy Tofu Scramble

Prep time: 15 minutes, Cook time: 7 minutes

Servings: 2

Ingredients:

- 1 cup firm silken tofu
- 1tsp. cayenne pepper
- 1tsp. chili paste
- 1tsp. soy sauce
- 1/2 tsp Salt

Preparation:

1. Spray a heat-proof bowl that fits in your Instant Pot with nonstick spray.
2. Chop the tofu finely. Stir in the remaining ingredients.
3. Pour into the bowl. Place the bowl in your steamer basket.
4. Pour 1 cup of water into your Instant Pot.
5. Lower the basket into your Instant Pot.
6. Seal and cook on low pressure for 7 minutes.
7. Depressurize quickly.
8. Stir well and allow to rest, it will finish cooking in its own heat.

Nutritional information:

Calories 582.6, Carbs 7g, Fat 3g, Protein 18g, Potassium (K) 424.2 mg, Sodium (Na) 717.6 mg

Breakfast Beans

Prep time: 15 minutes

Cook time: 10 minutes

Servings: 2

Ingredients:

- 1 lb. baked beans
- 1 lb. chopped mixed lean meats
- 1 cup scrambled eggs
- 1 tbsp. mixed herbs
- 2 stalks scallions

Preparation:

1. Mix all the ingredients in your Instant Pot, cook on Stew for 10 minutes.
2. Release the pressure naturally.

Nutritional information:

Calories 300, Carbs 29g, Fat 7g, Protein 42g, Potassium (K) 749 mg, Sodium (Na) 2.5 mg

Cheesy Eggs

Prep time: 15 minutes

Cook time: 7 minutes

Servings: 2

Ingredients:

- 3 eggs
- ¼ cup milk
- 2 tbsps. grated cheddar
- 1 tsp. mixed herbs
- 1/2 tsp. Salt

Preparation:

3. Spray a heat-proof bowl that fits in your Instant Pot with nonstick spray.
4. Whisk together the eggs, milk, salt, and herbs. Pour into the bowl.
5. Place the bowl in your steamer basket.
6. Pour 1 cup of water into your Instant Pot. Lower the basket into your Instant Pot.
7. Seal and cook on low pressure for 7 minutes. Depressurize quickly.
8. Add the cheese.
9. Stir well and allow to rest, it will finish cooking in its own heat.

Nutritional information:

Calories 100, Carbs 3g, Fat 8g, Protein 16g, Potassium (K) 193 mg, Sodium (Na) 451 mg

Eggs And Bacon

Prep time: 15 minutes

Cook time: 7 minutes

Serves: 2

Ingredients:

- 3 eggs
- ¼ cup milk
- ¼ cup chopped bacon
- 1 tsp. smoked paprika
- 1/2 tsp. Salt

Preparations:

1. Spray a heat-proof bowl that fits in your Instant Pot with nonstick spray.
2. Whisk the eggs and slowly add the other ingredients.
3. Pour into the bowl. Place the bowl in your steamer basket.
4. Pour 1 cup of water into your Instant Pot. Lower the basket into your Instant Pot.
5. Seal and cook on low pressure for 7 minutes. Depressurize quickly.
6. Stir well and allow to rest, it will finish cooking in its own heat.

Nutritional information:

Calories 230, Carbs 3g, Fat 12g, Protein 19g, Potassium (K)409.8 mg, Sodium (Na) 1030.3 mg

Eggs And Tomato

Prep time: 15 minutes

Cook time: 7 minutes

Servings: 2

Ingredients:

- 3 eggs
- ¼ cup milk
- 1 cup chopped cherry tomatoes
- 1 tsp. mixed herbs
- 1/2 tsp. Salt

Preparations:

1. Spray a heat-proof bowl that fits in your Instant Pot with nonstick spray.
2. Whisk together the eggs, milk, salt, and herbs.
3. Pour into the bowl. Add the tomatoes. Place the bowl in your steamer basket.
4. Pour 1 cup of water into your Instant Pot. Lower the basket into your Instant Pot.
5. Seal and cook on low pressure for 7 minutes. Depressurize quickly.
6. Stir well and allow to rest, it will finish cooking in its own heat.

Nutritional information:

Calories 110, Carbs 5g, Fat 8g, Protein 16g, Potassium (K)379 mg, Sodium (Na) 513 mg

Sausage Breakfast Casserole

Prep time: 15 minutes

Cook time: 10 minutes

Servings: 2

Ingredients:

- 1 lb. cooked chopped sausage
- 1 lb. chopped bell pepper and onions
- 1 cup low sodium broth
- 1 tbsp. mixed herbs
- 1 tbsp. Soy sauce

Preparation:

1. Mix all the ingredients in your Instant Pot, cook on Stew for 10 minutes.
2. Release the pressure naturally.

Nutritional information:

Calories 360, Carbs 10g, Fat 24g, Protein 35g, Potassium (K)307 mg, Sodium (Na) 755 mg

Hazelnut Chocolate Oats

Prep time: 10 minutes

Cook time: 5 minutes

Servings: 2

Ingredients:

- ½ cup high fiber steel cut oats
- 2 cups milk
- 4 tbsps. Hazelnuts
- 2 tbsps. Powdered sweetener
- 2 tbsps. dark chocolate chips

Preparation:

1. Pour the milk into your Instant Pot. Add the oats and sweetener, stir well.
2. Seal and close the vent. Choose Manual and set to cook 5 minutes.
3. Release the pressure naturally. Top with hazelnut and chocolate.

Nutritional information:

Calories 300, Carbs 25g, Fat 9g, Protein 12g, Potassium (K)75.3 mg, Sodium (Na) 135 mg

Eggs And Mushroom

Prep time: 15 minutes

Cook time: 7 minutes

Servings: 2

Ingredients:

- 3 eggs
- ¼ cup mushroom soup
- 1 cup chopped mushrooms
- 1 tsp. mixed herbs
- 1/2 tsp. Salt

Preparation:

1. Spray a heat-proof bowl that fits in your Instant Pot with nonstick spray.
2. Whisk together the eggs, soup, salt, and herbs.
3. Pour into the bowl. Add the mushrooms. Place the bowl in your steamer basket.
4. Pour 1 cup of water into your Instant Pot. Lower the basket into your Instant Pot.
5. Seal and cook on low pressure for 7 minutes. Depressurize quickly.
6. Stir well and allow to rest, it will finish cooking in its own heat.

Nutritional information:

Calories 100, Carbs 4g, Fat 8g, Protein 16g, Potassium (K)336 mg, Sodium (Na) 616 mg

Spanish Eggs

Prep time: 15 minutes

Cook time: 7 minutes

Servings: 2

Ingredients:

- 3 eggs
- ¼ cup milk
- 1 cup shredded, fried onion
- 1 tsp. smoked paprika
- 1/2 tsp. Salt

Preparations:

1. Spray a heat-proof bowl that fits in your Instant Pot with nonstick spray.
2. Whisk together the eggs, milk, salt, and paprika.
3. Pour into the bowl. Add the onion. Place the bowl in your steamer basket.
4. Pour 1 cup of water into your Instant Pot. Lower the basket into your Instant Pot.
5. Seal and cook on low pressure for 7 minutes. Depressurize quickly.
6. Stir well and allow to rest, it will finish cooking in its own heat.

Nutritional information:

Calories 125, Carbs 5g, Fat 8g, Protein 16g, Potassium (K) 1001 mg, Sodium (Na) 467.1 mg

Berry Oats

Prep time: 10 minutes

Cook time: 5 minutes

Servings: 2

Ingredients:

- ½ cup high fiber steel cut oats
- 2 cups milk
- 1 cup mixed berries

Preparations:

1. Pour the milk into your Instant Pot.
2. Add the oats, stir well.
3. Seal and close the vent.
4. Choose Manual and set to cook 5 minutes.
5. Release the pressure naturally.
6. Stir in the berries.

Nutritional information:

Calories 250, Carbs 19g, Fat 5g, Protein 6g, Potassium (K) 206.6 mg, Sodium (Na) 80.7 mg

Soups And Salads

Pumpkin Soup

Prep time: 15 minutes

Cook time: 10 minutes

Servings: 2

Ingredients:

- 1 lb. chopped pumpkin
- 1 lb. chopped tomato
- 1 cup broth
- 1 tbsp. mixed herbs
- 1 minced onion

Preparation:

1. Mix all the ingredients in your Instant Pot.
2. Cook on Stew for 10 minutes.
3. Release the pressure naturally.
4. Blend.

Nutritional information:

Calories 200, Carbs 7g, Fat 11g, Protein 2g, Potassium (K) 259 mg, Sodium (Na) 1033 mg

Beansprout Soup

Prep time: 15 minutes

Cook time: 10 minutes

Servings: 2

Ingredients:

- 1 lb. beansprouts
- 1 lb. chopped vegetables
- 1 cup low sodium broth
- 1 tbsp. mixed herbs
- 1 minced onion

Preparations:

1. Mix all the ingredients in your Instant Pot, cook on Stew for 10 minutes.
2. Release the pressure naturally and serve.

Nutritional information:

Calories 100, Carbs 4g, Fat 10g, Protein 4g, Potassium (K) 349.9 mg, Sodium (Na) 310 mg

Ham Hock Soup

Prep time: 15 minutes

Cook time: 10 minutes

Servings: 2

Ingredients:

- 1 lb. ham hock on the bone
- 1 lb. green peas
- 1 cup vegetable broth
- 1 cup shredded cabbage and onion
- 1 tbsp. mixed herbs

Preparations:

1. Mix all the ingredients in your Instant Pot, cook on Stew for 10 minutes.
2. Release the pressure naturally and serve.

Nutritional information:

Calories 200, Carbs 10g, Fat 15g, Protein 25g, Potassium (K) 484.3 mg, Sodium (Na) 296.3 mg

Egg Salad

Prep time: 5 minutes

Cook time: 5 minutes

Servings: 4

Ingredients:

- 8 eggs
- ¼ cup celery, diced
- ⅓ cup homemade mayonnaise
- 1 tsp. sea salt
- ½ tsp. black pepper
- Cooking oil spray

Preparation:

1. Lightly spray a baking or casserole dish with cooking oil spray and crack the eggs into the dish.
2. Place a wire steamer rack in the bottom of the Instant Pot and add a cup of water.
3. Place the baking dish on the rack and seal the Instant Pot lid.
4. Cook on the "Manual, High Pressure" setting for 5 minutes, and then release the steam manually when the cook cycle completes.
5. Remove the baking dish from the pot and slide the egg loaf onto a cutting board.
6. Chop and then combine with mayonnaise, celery, salt, and black pepper.
7. Chill until ready to serve.

Nutritional information:

Calories 266, Carbs 5.3g, Fat 22g, Protein 11g, Potassium (K) 137 mg, Sodium (Na) 714 mg

Wild Rice Salad With Cranberries And Almonds

Prep time: 10 minutes

Cook time: 25 minutes

Servings: 8

Ingredients:

For the rice

- 2 cups wild rice
- 1 tsp. kosher salt
- 2½ cups Vegetable Broth
- 1 juiced orange
- 1 tsp. honey

For the salad

- ¾ cup unsweetened dried cranberries
- ½ cup sliced almonds
- Black pepper

For the dressing

- ¼ cup extra-virgin olive oil
- ¼ cup white wine vinegar
- 1½ tsps. grated orange zest

Preparations:

1. In the electric pressure cooker, combine the rice, salt, and broth.
2. Close and lock the lid. Set the valve to sealing, cook on high pressure for 25 minutes.
3. When the cooking is complete, hit Cancel and allow the pressure to release naturally for 15 minutes, then quick release any remaining pressure.
4. Once the pin drops, unlock and remove the lid.
5. Let the rice cool briefly, then fluff it with a fork.

To make the dressing

6. In a small jar with a screw-top lid, combine the olive oil, vinegar, zest, juice, and honey. (If you don't have a jar, whisk the ingredients together in a small bowl.) Shake to combine.

To make the salad

7. In a large bowl, combine the rice, cranberries, and almonds.
8. Add the dressing and season with pepper.
9. Serve warm or refrigerate.

Nutritional information:

Calories 126, Carbs 18g, Fat 5g, Protein 3g, Potassium (K) 91.4 mg, Sodium (Na) 120 mg

Strawberry Farro Salad

Prep time: 17 minutes

Cook time: 10 minutes

Servings: 8

Ingredients:

For the farro

- 1 cup drained farro
- ¼ tsp. kosher salt
- ½ tsp. poppy seeds
- ¼ cup extra-virgin olive oil

For the dressing

- 1 tbsp. squeezed lime juice
- ½ tbsp. fruit-flavored balsamic vinegar
- ½ tsp. Dijon mustard
- ½ tbsp. honey

For the salad

- 1¼ cups sliced strawberries
- ¼ cup slivered almonds
- Black pepper
- Fresh basil leaves

Preparations:

To make the farro

1. In the electric pressure cooker, combine the farro, salt, and 2 cups of water.
2. Close and lock the lid. Set the valve to sealing, cook on high pressure for 10 minutes.
3. When the cooking is complete, allow the pressure to release naturally for 10 minutes, then quick release the remaining pressure. Hit Cancel.
4. Once the pin drops, unlock and remove the lid.
5. Fluff the farro with a fork and let cool.

To make the dressing

6. In a small jar with a screw-top lid, combine the lime juice, balsamic vinegar, mustard, honey, poppy seeds, and olive oil. Shake until well combined.

To make the salad

7. In a large bowl, toss the farro with the dressing. Stir in the strawberries and almonds.
8. Season with pepper, garnish with basil, and serve.

Nutritional information:

Calories 176, Carbs 22g, Fat 9g, Protein 3g, Sugar 6.4, Sodium (Na) 68 mg

Wheat Berry, Black Bean, And Avocado Salad

Prep time: 10 minutes

Cook time: 30 minutes

Servings: 4

Ingredients:

- 1/3 cup dried black beans
- ½ cup wheat berries
- 1 chopped avocado
- 2 cups grape tomatoes
- 1 cup chopped poblano pepper
- ½ cup chopped cilantro
- 1 tsp. minced garlic
- ½ tsp. salt
- 4 cups water
- 2 tbsps. apple cider vinegar
- 2 tbsps. olive oil
- 3 oz. shredded cheddar cheese

Preparations:

1. Plugin instant pot, insert the inner pot, add black beans and wheat berries and then pour in water.
2. Press the cancel button, shut the instant pot with its lid and turn the pressure knob to seal the pot.
3. Press the 'manual' button, then press the 'timer' to set the cooking time to 25 minutes and cook at high pressure, instant pot will take 5 minutes or more for building its inner pressure.
4. Meanwhile, place tomato and pepper in a bowl, add garlic and cilantro, season with salt, then drizzle with vinegar and oil and stir until mixed.
5. When the timer beeps, press 'cancel' button, do quick pressure release until pressure nob drops down.
6. Open the instant pot, drain the wheat and berries, rinse under cold water, then drain well and place in a large bowl.
7. Add tomato and pepper mixture, then add avocado and cheese and toss until evenly mixed.
8. Serve straight away.

Nutritional information:

Calories 320, Carbs 33g, Fat 17g, Protein 13g, Potassium (K) 740 mg, Sodium (Na) 480 mg

Chickpea Salad

Prep time: 5 minutes

Cook time: 40 minutes

Servings: 6

Ingredients:

- 1 cup dried chickpeas
- 3 cups water
- ¼ cup chopped green bell pepper
- 10 halved black olives
- 10 halved cherry tomatoes
- 2 tbsps. chopped cilantro
- 1 diced cucumber
- ½ cup chopped white onion
- 2 tbsps. crumbled feta cheese

For Dressing:

- 1 tsp. salt
- ½ tsp. black pepper
- 1 tbsp. red wine vinegar
- 2 tbsps. olive oil

Preparations:

1. Plugin instant pot, insert the inner pot, add chickpeas, and pour in water.
2. Shut the instant pot with its lid, turn the pressure knob to seal the pot, press the 'manual' button, then press the 'timer' to set the cooking time to 35 minutes and cook at high pressure, instant pot will take 5 minutes or more for building its inner pressure.
3. Meanwhile, whisk together all the ingredients for the dressing and set aside until required.
4. When the timer beeps, press 'cancel' button and do quick pressure release until pressure nob drops down.
5. Open the instant pot, drain the chickpeas, let cool for 20 minutes and then transfer into a salad bowl.
6. Drizzle chickpeas with prepared salad dressing, then add remaining ingredients and toss until well coated.
7. Chill salad in the refrigerator for 30 minutes and then serve.

Nutritional information:

Calories 301, Carbs 37g, Fat 13g, Protein 11g, Potassium (K) 319 mg, Sodium (Na) 500 mg

Taco Soup

Prep time: 15 minutes

Cook time: 15 minutes

Servings: 4

Ingredients:

- 1 tbsp. olive oil
- 1 diced yellow onion
- 2 minced garlic cloves
- 15 oz. drained black beans
- 14 oz. crushed tomatoes
- 1 cup frozen sweetcorn
- 3 diced bell peppers
- 6 cups vegetable broth
- 1 box chickpea pasta shells
- 1 sliced jalapeño pepper, sliced
- 1 tbsp. chili powder
- 1 tsp. ground cumin
- 1 tsp. dried oregano
- ½ tsp. sea salt

To Serve:

- Fresh cilantro
- 1 sliced avocado

Preparation:

1. Add the olive oil, onions, garlic, tomatoes, corn, beans, spices and vegetable broth to Instant Pot. Stir gently.
2. Cover and seal the lid, making sure the steam release valve is set to "Sealing."
3. Cook on the "Manual, High Pressure" setting for 3 minutes, and once done, do a quick release of the pressure.
4. Stir in the diced bell peppers and chickpeas pasta, and then sit for 5-10 minutes.
5. Ladle the soup into bowls, top with the diced jalapeño, fresh cilantro and sliced avocados, and then serve.

Nutritional information:

Calories 430, Carbs 74g, Fat 9g, Protein 27g, Potassium (K) 620 mg, Sodium (Na) 921 mg

Tomato And Cheddar Soup

Prep time: 5 minutes

Cook time: 10 minutes

Servings: 6

Ingredients:

- 2 tbsps. avocado oil
- ½ cup white onion, chopped
- 1 chopped celery stalk
- 1 lb. chopped tomatoes
- 4 cups low-sodium chicken broth
- 2 minced garlic cloves
- ½ tsp. dried thyme
- 6 oz. shredded Cheddar cheese
- 4 oz. cream cheese
- 1 tsp. Sea salt
- Black pepper

Preparations:

1. Select the "Sauté" function on the Instant Pot, and add the oil.
2. Once the oil is hot, add the onions and celery, and season with salt and black pepper.
3. Sauté for 4 minutes until tender.
4. Add the garlic and the thyme, and sauté for another minute or so, and then add the tomatoes, cream cheese, and broth.
5. Close and seal the lid, and cook on the "Manual, High Pressure" setting for 10 minutes.
6. Once the cook cycle is up, allow for a natural pressure release for 10 more minutes.
7. Release all the remaining pressure in the pot, and then carefully remove the lid.
8. Add the shredded Cheddar cheese, and then hand-blend the soup with an immersion blender, until velvety and smooth.
9. Season to your preference and serve.

Nutritional information:

Calories 233, Carbs 6.54g, Fat 18.62g, Protein 11.04g, Potassium (K) 0 mg, Sodium (Na) 690 mg

Vegetable Dishes

Steamed Asparagus

Prep time: 3 minutes

Cook time: 2 minutes

Servings: 4

Ingredients:

- 1 lb. fresh asparagus, rinsed and tough ends trimmed
- 1 cup water

Preparation:

1. Place the asparagus into a wire steamer rack, and set it inside your Instant Pot.
2. Add water to the pot. Close and seal the lid, turning the steam release valve to the "Sealing" position.
3. Select the "Steam" function to cook on high pressure for 2 minutes.
4. Once done, do a quick pressure release of the steam.
5. Lift the wire steamer basket out of the pot and place the asparagus onto a serving plate.
6. Season as desired and serve.

Nutritional information:

Calories 22, Carbs 4g, Fat 0 g, Protein 2g, Potassium (K) 229 mg, Sodium (Na) 5 mg

Lentil And Eggplant Stew

Prep time: 15 minutes

Cook time: 35 minutes

Servings: 2

Ingredients:

- 1 lb. eggplant
- 1 lb. dry lentils
- 1 cup chopped vegetables
- 1 cup low sodium vegetable broth

Preparation:

1. Mix all the ingredients in your Instant Pot, cook on Stew for 35 minutes.
2. Release the pressure naturally and serve.

Nutritional information:

Calories 310, Carbs 22g, Fat 10g, Protein 32g, Potassium (K) 670.6 mg, Sodium (Na) 267 mg

Squash Medley

Prep time: 10 minutes.

Cook time: 20 minutes.

Servings: 2

Ingredients:

- 2 lbs. mixed squash
- ½ cup mixed veg
- 1 cup vegetable stock
- 2 tbsps. olive oil
- 2 tbsps. mixed herbs

Preparation:

1. Put the squash in the steamer basket and add the stock into the Instant Pot.
2. Steam the squash in your Instant Pot for 10 minutes.
3. Depressurize and pour away the remaining stock.
4. Set to sauté and add the oil and remaining ingredients.
5. Cook until a light crust forms.

Nutritional information:

Calories 100, Carbs 10g, Fat 6g, Protein 5g, Potassium (K) 399.2 mg, Sodium (Na) 478.9 mg

Eggplant Curry

Prep time: 15 minutes

Cook time: 20 minutes

Servings: 2

Ingredients:

- 3 cups chopped eggplant
- 1 thinly sliced onion
- 1 cup coconut milk
- 3 tbsps. curry paste
- 1 tbsp. oil or ghee

Preparation:

1. Set the Instant Pot to sauté and add the onion, oil, and curry paste.
2. When the onion is soft, add the remaining ingredients and seal.
3. Cook on Stew for 20 minutes. Release the pressure naturally.

Nutritional information:

Calories 350, Carbs 15g, Fat 25g, Protein 11g, Potassium (K) 800.6 mg, Sodium (Na) 728.6 mg

Tofu Curry

Prep time: 15 minutes

Cook time: 20 minutes

Servings: 2

Ingredients:

- 2 cups cubed extra firm tofu
- 2 cups mixed stir fry vegetables
- ½ cup soy yogurt
- 3 tbsps. curry paste
- 1 tbsp. oil or ghee

Preparation:

1. Set the Instant Pot to sauté and add the oil and curry paste.
2. When the onion is soft, add the remaining ingredients except for the yogurt and seal.
3. Cook on Stew for 20 minutes.
4. Release the pressure naturally and serve with a scoop of soy yogurt.

Nutritional information:

Calories 300, Carbs 9g, Fat 14g, Protein 42g, Potassium (K) 779.6 mg, Sodium (Na) 902.1 mg

Lentil And Chickpea Curry

Prep time: 15 minutes

Cook time: 20 minutes

Servings: 2

Ingredients:

- 2 cups dry lentils and chickpeas
- 1 thinly sliced onion
- 1 cup chopped tomato
- 3 tbsps. curry paste
- 1 tbsp. oil or ghee

Preparation:

1. Set the Instant Pot to sauté and add the onion, oil, and curry paste.
2. When the onion is soft, add the remaining ingredients and seal.
3. Cook on Stew for 20 minutes.
4. Release the pressure naturally and serve.

Nutritional information:

Calories 360, Carbs 26g, Fat 19g, Protein 23g, Potassium (K) 866.5 mg, Sodium (Na) 964.4mg

Split Pea Stew

Prep time: 5 minutes

Cook time: 35 minutes

Servings: 2

Ingredients:

- 1 cup dry split peas
- 1 lb. chopped vegetables
- 1 cup mushroom soup
- 2 tbsps. old bay seasoning

Preparation:

1. Mix all the ingredients in your Instant Pot, cook on Beans for 35 minutes.
2. Release the pressure naturally.

Nutritional information:

Calories 300, Carbs 7g, Fat 2g, Protein 24g, Potassium (K) 63.2 mg, Sodium (Na) 797.7 mg

Kidney Bean Stew

Prep time: 15 minutes

Cook time: 15 minutes

Servings: 2

Ingredients:

- 1 lb. cooked kidney beans
- 1 cup tomato passata
- 1 cup low sodium beef broth
- 3 tbsps. Italian herbs

Preparation:

1. Mix all the ingredients in your Instant Pot, cook on Stew for 15 minutes.
2. Release the pressure naturally and serve.

Nutritional information:

Calories 270, Carbs 16g, Fat 10g, Protein 23g, Potassium (K) 663.5 mg, Sodium (Na) 641.2 mg

Fried Tofu Hotpot

Prep time: 15 minutes

Cook time: 15 minutes

Servings: 2

Ingredients:

- ½ lb. fried tofu
- 1 lb. chopped Chinese vegetable mix
- 1 cup low sodium vegetable broth
- 2 tbsps. 5 spice seasoning
- 1 tbsp. smoked paprika

Preparation:

1. Mix all the ingredients in your Instant Pot, cook on Stew for 15 minutes.
2. Release the pressure naturally and serve.

Nutritional information:

Calories 320, Carbs 11g, Fat 23g, Protein 47g, Potassium (K) 98.1 mg, Sodium (Na) 456 mg

Chili Sin Carne

Prep time: 15 minutes

Cook time: 35 minutes

Servings: 2

Ingredients:

- 3 cups mixed cooked beans
- 2 cups chopped tomatoes
- 1 tbsp. yeast extract
- 2 squares very dark chocolate
- 1 tbsp. red chili flakes

Preparation:

1. Mix all the ingredients in your Instant Pot, cook on Beans for 35 minutes.
2. Release the pressure naturally and serve.

Nutritional information:

Calories 240, Carbs 20g, Fat 3g, Protein 36g, Potassium (K) 0 mg, Sodium (Na) 2 mg

Meatless Main Dish

Wild Rice Pilaf

Prep Time: 10 min

Cook Time: 50 min

Servings: 8

Ingredients:

- 2 tbsp. olive oil
- 2 cups wild rice brown basmati blend
- 2 cups vegetable stock
- 2 chopped brown onions
- 2 minced garlic cloves
- 12 oz. sliced mushrooms
- ½ tsp. dried thyme
- ¼ cup dry white wine
- ½ tsp. sea salt

To Serve:

- ½ cup pine nuts or slivered almond
- ½ cup chopped parsley

Preparations:

1. Select the 'Sauté' function on a large 6-quart Instant Pot.
2. Heat the olive oil, and add the onions, cook for 5-7 minutes, until softened and translucent.
3. Add in the garlic and sauté for 1 minute.
4. Next, add ¼ cup of white wine, or vegetable stock and deglaze the Instant Pot for up to 2 minutes.
5. Cancel the 'Sauté' function on the Instant Pot and add all the remaining ingredients. Stir well to combine.
6. Cook on the "Manual, High Pressure" for 28 minutes, and then allow for a natural pressure release for 15 minutes, and then do a manual pressure release to remove any remaining pressure.
7. Carefully open the lid and stir in the parsley and pine nuts. Serve immediately and enjoy.
8. To reheat the pilaf, pre-heat the oven to 350F.
9. Add the pilaf to a casserole dish, and bake, covered, for 30 minutes, or until heated through.
10. Stir in the toasted pine nuts and fresh parsley, and serve.

Nutritional information:

Calories 263, Carbs 36g, Fat 9g, Protein 8g, Potassium (K) 427 mg, Sodium (Na) 389 mg

Vegetable And Brown Rice Stuffed Bell Peppers

Prep Time: 25 min

Cook Time: 1 hr.

Servings: 8

Ingredients:

- 2 cups cooked brown rice
- 8 bell peppers
- ½ cup grated Parmesan cheese
- 1 minced shallot
- 2 minced stalks celery
- 1 shredded carrot
- ½ cup chopped black olives
- 2 oz. crumbled goat cheese
- 15 oz. rinsed chickpeas
- ⅓ cup chopped sun-dried tomatoes
- ¼ cup chopped parsley, chopped
- 3 tbsp. fresh lemon juice
- 2 tbsps. oil reserved from the sun-dried tomatoes jar
- 2 tsps. dried oregano
- 2 tsps. Dried basil
- 1½ tsp. garlic powder
- ¾ tsp. sea salt
- ¼ tsps. black pepper
- ¼ tsp. red pepper flakes

Preparation:

1. In a large mixing bowl, combine the chickpeas, rice, carrots, celery, shallot, olives, crumbled goat's cheese, sun-dried tomatoes, lemon juice, parsley, oregano, basil, garlic powder, black pepper, salt, and pepper flakes.
2. Trim the bottoms of the peppers without to stabilize them, without cutting through bottoms.
3. Top each pepper and then remove the seeds and ribs.
4. Apportion the rice filling evenly into the peppers. Drizzle with the reserved oil from the sun-dried tomatoes.
5. Place the stuffed peppers into 2 large glass containers or freezer bags, and freeze them.
6. When ready to serve and eat, pour a cup of water into the Instant Pot, and place a wire steamer rack on top.
7. Place 4 stuffed peppers onto the rack.
8. Lock and seal the lid and make sure the pressure release valve is set to "Sealing."
9. Cook on the "Manual, High Pressure" setting for 8 minutes, and once done, leave the vent in the seal position, while allowing all the pressure to release naturally.
10. Carefully uncover the lid, sprinkle the peppers with grated Parmesan, and serve.

Nutritional information:

Calories 241, Carbs 32g, Fat 10g, Protein 8g, Potassium (K) 721.8 mg, Sodium (Na) 416 mg

Asparagus Risotto

Prep time: 5 minutes

Cook time: 25 minutes

Servings: 6

Ingredients:

- 1 tbsp. extra-virgin olive oil
- 1½ cups Arborio rice
- 1 lb. asparagus
- 1 chopped shallot
- 1 minced garlic clove
- 3 cups vegetable broth
- ½ cup sliced shiitake mushrooms
- ⅓ cup dry white wine
- ¼ cup grated Fontina cheese
- 2 tbsps. grated Parmesan cheese
- 1 tbsp. butter
- 2 tsps. fresh thyme leaves
- 1 tsp. lemon zest
- 1 tsp. sea salt
- ¼ tsp. ground black pepper

Preparation:

1. Select the "Sauté" function on the Instant Pot and add the olive oil.
2. Once hot, add the shallots and garlic, stirring and cooking for approximately 1 minute.
3. Add the Arborio rice, and cook for 2 minutes until the rice is slightly translucent.
4. Pour in the dry wine and deglaze the bottom of the pan.
5. Add the broth, and then close and seal the lid.
6. Close the vent cook on the "Manual, High Pressure" setting for 7 minutes.
7. Sauté the mushrooms in a large skillet in 1 tablespoon of olive oil for 5-6 minutes on the stove top.
8. Add the asparagus and cook for 3-5 minutes.
9. Once done, do a quick release and then hit the "Cancel" button to turn off the Instant Pot.
10. Stir in the lemon zest, thyme, Parmesan and Fontina cheeses, butter, and the sautéed mushrooms and asparagus.
11. Adjust the consistency of the broth and stir.

Nutritional information:

Calories 287, Carbs 46g, Fat 6g, Protein 7g, Potassium (K) 271 mg, Sodium (Na) 949 mg

Stuffed Sweet Potatoes

Prep time: 15 min

Cook time: 20 min

Servings: 4

Ingredients:

- Olive oil
- 2 medium sweet potatoes
- 2 spring onions
- 1 cup cooked chickpeas
- 1 cup cooked couscous
- 1 avocado
- 1 whole lemon
- 3 oz. feta cheese
- 1 tsp. paprika
- Black pepper
- 1 tsp. sea salt

Preparation:

1. Wash and scrub the sweet potatoes under clean running water. Pierce with a fork or knife.
2. Pour 1½ cups water into the Instant Pot and insert a wire steamer rack into the pot.
3. Place the sweet potatoes onto the rack and then lock the lid, turning the steam release valve to "Sealing."
4. Press the "Manual, High Pressure" setting and cook for 17 minutes.
5. On the stove top pan-roast the drained chickpeas with some olive oil, and then season with salt and pepper.
6. Once the chickpeas start to brown, add the paprika and stir until the chickpeas are evenly coated.
7. Pan-fry for a 1 minute before turning off the heat.
8. Now chop the spring onions, and then peel and halve the avocado. Remove the stone and slice.
9. Once the sweet potatoes are done, allow for a natural pressure release.
10. Turn off the Instant Pot and open the lid.
11. Halve the potatoes (but not all the way through) and mash the flesh with a fork.
12. Add the toppings and serve with lemon wedges and crumbled feta cheese.

Nutritional information:

Calories 776, Carbs 117g, Fat 26g, Protein 23g, Potassium (K) 1942 mg, Sodium (Na) 660 mg

Couscous Tomatoes

Prep time: 20 minutes

Cook time: 18 minutes

Servings: 8

Ingredients:

- ½ cup uncooked couscous
- 8 large tomatoes
- 1 diced eggplant
- ½ cup chopped apricots
- ½ cup sliced almonds
- 1½ tsps. salt
- ¾ tsp. ground black pepper
- ½ tsp. ground cumin
- 1 tsp. ground coriander
- 1/8 tsp. ground cinnamon
- 2 tbsps. chopped mint
- 1 tbsp. olive oil
- 1 tsp. harissa paste
- 1 cup vegetable broth

Preparation:

1. Cut off tomato from the top, then scoop out the seeds and sprinkle the hollow inside with some salt.
2. Then place tomatoes onto a paper towel-lined plate and set aside until tomatoes are drained.
3. Meanwhile, plug-in instant pot, insert the inner pot, press sauté/simmer button and when hot, add ½ tablespoon oil and almonds and cook for 2 to 4 minutes or until nicely golden brown.
4. Transfer almonds to a plate and set aside, then add remaining oil along with eggplant pieces and cook for 5 minutes or until nicely browned on all sides.
5. Season eggplant with cinnamon, cumin, coriander, then cook for 30 seconds or until fragrant, add couscous and stir well.
6. Press the cancel button, pour in the broth, then shut the instant pot with its lid and turn the pressure knob to seal the pot.
7. Press the 'manual' button, then press the 'timer' to set the cooking time to 2 minutes and cook at high pressure, instant pot will take 5 minutes or more for building its inner pressure.
8. When the timer beeps, press 'cancel' button and do natural pressure release for 10 minutes or until pressure nob drops down.
9. Open the instant pot, then fluff couscous with a fork, add apricots, cooked almonds and mint and stir until combined.
10. Pour harissa paste over couscous, season with salt and black pepper and spoon the mixture into hollowed tomatoes.
11. Serve immediately.

Nutritional information:

Calories 175, Carbs 28g, Fat 6g, Protein 5g, Potassium (K) 138.3 mg, Sodium (Na) 45.8 mg

Barley Pilaf With Tofu

Prep time: 10 minutes

Cook time: 30 minutes , Servings: 4

Ingredients:

- 4 oz. pearl barley
- ¼ tsp. white pepper
- 1 tsp. ground cumin
- 1 tsp. ground cinnamon
- 1 ¾ cups vegetable broth
- 4 tsps. olive oil
- 6 oz. sliced firm tofu
- 1 tsp. minced garlic
- 1 tsp. grated ginger
- ½ tsp. Chinese five-spice mix
- 1 tbsp. chopped coriander
- 1 sliced red onion
- 1 diced zucchini
- 1 chopped red bell pepper
- 1 chopped yellow bell pepper
- 4oz. frozen peas
- 2 tsps. soy sauce
- 3 oz. pomegranate seeds

Preparations:

1. Plugin instant pot, insert the inner pot, add barley, stir in white pepper, cumin, and cinnamon, and then pour in broth.
2. Shut the instant pot with its lid and turn the pressure knob to seal the pot.
3. Press the 'manual' button, then press the 'timer' to set the cooking time to 20 minutes and cook at high pressure, instant pot will take 5 minutes or more for building its inner pressure.
4. Meanwhile, place a skillet pan over medium heat, add 2 teaspoons oil and when hot, add tofu slices and cook for 5 to 7 minutes or until nicely browned on all sides.
5. When done, transfer tofu pieces to a cutting board, then let them cool and cut into small pieces, set aside until required.
6. Return skillet pan over medium heat, add garlic and ginger and cook for 1 to 2 minutes or until fragrant.
7. Return tofu pieces into the pan, season with five-spice mix, add ½ tablespoon coriander, stir well and transfer tofu to a bowl, set aside until required.
8. When the timer beeps, press 'cancel' button and do quick pressure release until pressure nob drops down.
9. Open the instant pot and stir barley and check it, barley must be tender.
10. Return skillet pan over medium heat, add remaining oil in it, then add onion, zucchini, and peppers and cook for 5 to 6 minutes or until softened.
11. Add peas and cooked barley mixture and stir well.
12. Divide barley evenly between serving plates, top with tofu, garnish with coriander, then drizzle with soy sauce and scatter pomegranate seeds on top.
13. Serve straight away.

Nutritional information:

Calories 571, Carbs 77g, Fat 15g, Protein 23.6g, Potassium (K) 337.2 mg, Sodium (Na) 954.1 mg

Black and Pinto Bean Chili

Prep time: 15 minutes

Cook time: 4 hours

Servings: 8

Ingredients:

- 1 lb. ground turkey
- 14.5 oz. cooked black beans
- 14.5 oz. cooked pinto beans
- 1 chopped green pepper
- 28 oz. diced tomatoes
- 1 chopped white onion
- 1 tsp. minced garlic
- 1½ tsps. black pepper
- 1 tsp. chopped oregano
- 1½ tsps. cayenne pepper
- ½ tsp. cumin
- 1 cup vegetable stock

Preparations:

1. Plugin instant pot, insert the inner pot, press sauté/simmer button and when hot, add turkey along with remaining ingredients and stir until mixed.
2. Shut the instant pot with its lid and turn the pressure knob to seal the pot.
3. Press the 'slow cook' button, then press the 'timer' to set the cooking time to 4 hours at low heat setting.
4. When the timer beeps, press 'cancel' button and do natural pressure release for 10 minutes and then do quick pressure release until pressure nob drops down.
5. Open the instant pot, stir the chili and then evenly divide into serving bowls.
6. Serve straight away.

Nutritional information:

Calories 217, Carbs 26.8g, Fat 4.8g, Protein 18.9g, Potassium (K) 743.8 mg, Sodium (Na) 509.5 mg

Black Beans, Corn, and Cheese on Sweet Potato

Prep time: 20 minutes

Cook time: 15 minutes

Servings: 6

Ingredients:

- 6 medium sweet potato
- 14 oz. cooked black beans
- 15.25 oz. cooked corn
- 1/3 cup shredded sharp cheddar
- 1 cup water

Preparations:

1. Plugin instant pot, insert the inner pot, pour in water, then insert steamer basket and place sweet potatoes on it.
2. Shut the instant pot with its lid and turn the pressure knob to seal the pot.
3. Press the 'steam' button, then press the 'timer' to set the cooking time to 10 minutes and cook at high pressure, instant pot will take 5 minutes or more for building its inner pressure.
4. When the timer beeps, press 'cancel' button and do natural pressure release or until pressure nob drops down.
5. Then open the instant pot, remove sweet potatoes, and let cool enough to be handled by hands.
6. Peel the sweet potatoes, cut into bite-size pieces, then place in a bowl and mash with form until smooth.
7. Divide mashed sweet potatoes evenly between six plates, evenly top with beans and corn and sprinkle with cheese.
8. Serve straight away.

Nutritional information:

Calories 194, Carbs 61.5g, Fat 3.1g, Protein 9.6g, Potassium (K) 950 mg, Sodium (Na) 265.5 mg

Chick Pea Curry

Prep time: 10 minutes

Cook time: 27 minutes

Servings: 2

Ingredients:

- 1 cup chickpeas, uncooked
- 1 chopped white onion
- 2 chopped green chilies
- 1 chopped tomato
- 2 tsps. minced garlic
- 1 tsp. grated ginger
- 1 tsp. salt
- 1 tsp. red chili powder
- 1 tsp. coriander powder
- 1 tsp. garam masala
- 1 tsp. turmeric powder
- 3 bay leaves
- 3 tbsps. olive oil
- 1 tbsp. chopped parsley
- 2 cups water

Preparation:

1. Plugin instant pot, insert the inner pot, and add chickpeas and 1 ¼ cup water.
2. Shut the instant pot with its lid and turn the pressure knob to seal the pot.
3. Press the 'manual' button, then press the 'timer' to set the cooking time to 12 minutes and cook at high pressure, instant pot will take 5 minutes or more for building its inner pressure.
4. When the timer beeps, press 'cancel' button and do natural pressure release for 5 minutes and then do quick pressure release until pressure nob drops down.
5. Then open the instant pot, drain chickpeas, and set aside.
6. Place a skillet pan over medium heat, add oil and bay leaves and fry for 30 seconds.
7. Stir in ginger and garlic paste and cook for 1 minute or until nicely golden brown and fragrant.
8. Season with salt, chili powder, coriander, garam masala, and turmeric, continue cooking for 3 minutes, then pour in remaining water and bring the gravy to boil.
9. Then add cooked chickpeas, stir well, and cook for 5 minutes, covering the pan.
10. Serve straight away.

Nutritional information:

Calories 212, Carbs 39g, Fat 3.6g, Protein 9.8g, Potassium (K) 387 mg, Sodium (Na) 836 mg

Yellow Lentils

Prep time: 10 minutes
Cook time: 20 minutes
Servings: 4

Ingredients:

- ½ cup yellow lentils
- 1 green chili, chopped
- ½ tsp. salt
- ½ tsp. mustard seeds
- ½ tsp. cumin seeds
- ½ juiced lemon
- 1 tbsp. olive oil
- 2 cups water
- 1 tbsp. chopped cilantro

Preparations:

1. Plugin instant pot, insert the inner pot, add lentils and pour in 1 cup water.
2. Shut the instant pot with its lid and turn the pressure knob to seal the pot.
3. Press the 'manual' button, then press the 'timer' to set the cooking time to 5 minutes and cook at high pressure, instant pot will take 5 minutes or more for building its inner pressure.
4. When the timer beeps, press 'cancel' button and do natural pressure release for 5 minutes and then do quick pressure release until pressure nob drops down.
5. Open the instant pot, add salt, green chilies and remaining water and stir until mixed.
6. Press the 'sauté/simmer' button and cook lentils for 5 minutes or more until boil.
7. Meanwhile, place a skillet pan over medium heat, add oil and when hot, add cumin seeds and mustard seeds and cook for 1 to 2 minutes or until fragrant.
8. Carefully, add seed mixture into lentils and press the cancel button.
9. Add lemon juice, stir well and then garnish with cilantro.
10. Serve straight away.

Nutritional information:

Calories 55.6, Carbs 6.2g, Fat 2.6g, Protein 2.5g, Potassium (K) 497.8 mg, Sodium (Na) 889.7 mg

Beef Pork And Lamb

Pork Carnitas

Prep time: 5 min

Cook time: 85 min

Servings: 4

Ingredients:

- 2 ½ lbs. boneless pork shoulder roast
- 6 garlic cloves
- 1 cup low-sodium chicken broth
- 2 bay leaves
- 3 chipotle peppers in adobo sauce
- 2 tsps. kosher salt
- 1½ tsps. ground cumin
- ½ tsp. sazon
- ½ tsp. garlic powder
- ¼ tsp. dry adobo seasoning
- ¼ tsp. dried oregano
- Coarsely ground black pepper
- Cooking oil spray

Preparation:

1. Season the pork with black pepper and salt, and set aside.
2. Select the "Sauté" function on the Instant Pot, spray with cooking oil and sear the pork for about 5 minutes. Remove the pork once done, set aside, and allow to cool.
3. With a sharp knife, cut slits into the pork, and insert the thin garlic slivers all over the pork to flavor it.
4. Season the pork with sazon, cumin, oregano, adobo and garlic powder.
5. Pour in the chicken broth, add the chipotle peppers and stir. Then add the bay leaves and return the pork into the Instant Pot.
6. Cover and seal the Instant Pot making sure the pressure valve is set to "Sealing."
7. Cook on the "Manual, High Pressure" setting for 80 minutes.
8. Once the pork is cooked and you have released all the pressure, shred the pork using two forks and combine with the cooking juices at the bottom of the pot.
9. Remove and discard the bay leaves, adjust the cumin and adobo to your taste, mix well, and serve.

Nutritional information:

Calories 160, Carbs 1g, Fat 7 g, Protein 20g, Potassium (K) 305 mg, Sodium (Na) 397 mg

Lamb Shoulder

Prep time: 15 min

Cook time: 1 hr. 30 min

Servings: 6

Ingredients:

- 2 tsp. good olive oil
- 4 lbs. bone-in lamb shoulder
- 2 cups low-sodium beef or chicken stock
- 1 sprig fresh rosemary
- 6 chopped anchovies
- 1 tsp. garlic purée
- 1 tsp. dried oregano
- 1 1/2 tsps. Kosher salt

Preparation:

1. Select the "Sauté" function on your Instant Pot and add oil.
2. Once hot, add the lamb shoulder and sear until nicely browned. Set aside for now.
3. Add the chicken stock to deglaze the bottom of the pan and then stir in the anchovies and garlic.
4. Return the lamb to the Instant Pot insert, sprinkle with salt and oregano, and then add the rosemary sprig.
5. Cover and seal the Instant Pot, turning the pressure valve to "Sealing."
6. Cook on the "Manual, High Pressure" setting for 1½ hours.
7. Once done, allow for a 15-minute natural pressure release and then do a quick pressure release to release any remaining steam.
8. Slice and serve with your favorite side.

Nutritional information:

Calories 300, Carbs 3g, Fat 12 g, Protein 40g, Potassium (K) 646 mg, Sodium (Na) 250 mg

Beef Bourguignon Stew

Prep time: 30 min

Cook time: 30 min

Servings: 6

Ingredients:

- 1 tbsp. butter or olive oil
- 1½ lbs. diced stewing meat
- 4 slices bacon, sliced
- 1 small white onion, diced
- 1 clove garlic, crushed
- 2 stalks celery, sliced
- 8 oz. mushrooms, sliced
- 1 cup low-sodium beef stock
- 1 cup good-quality dry red wine
- 2 tbsp. tomato paste
- 1 bay leaf
- ½ tsp. dried thyme
- ½ tsp. xanthan gum
- ½ tsp. sea salt, or to taste)
- ¼ tsp. freshly ground black pepper
- 1 tbsp. fresh parsley chopped

Preparation:

1. Select the "Sauté" function on your Instant Pot and sauté the bacon until crispy.
2. Once done, set aside and reserve the bacon grease in the pot.
3. Sear the beef in the Instant Pot, working in batches to avoid overcrowding the pot and stewing the beef.
4. Discard all but a tablespoon of the drippings from the pot, and add a tablespoon of butter or preferred cooking oil.
5. Sauté the onions and celery to the pot, until soft and then add the mushrooms.
6. Stir in the garlic and cook for one minute.
7. Remove all the vegetables and set aside on a side plate.
8. Add xanthan gum to the Instant Pot, followed by the wine; deglaze the pot thoroughly.
9. Simmer until the wine begins to thicken, and then add the beef broth.
10. Stir in the tomato paste, bay leaf, and thyme, and simmer until the sauce is sufficiently reduced.
11. Return the sautéed vegetables, beef, and bacon to the pot. Stir in the salt and black pepper.
12. Cover and seal the Instant Pot, making sure the steam release handle is pointed to "Sealing."
13. Select the "Meat/Stew" function and adjust to cook for 30 minutes.
14. Once done, do a quick pressure release and uncover the stew.
15. Taste and adjust for seasoning, remove and discard the bay leaf and garnish with parsley prior to serving.

Nutritional information:

Calories 324, Carbs 5g, Fat 18 g, Protein 28g, Potassium (K) 766 mg, Sodium (Na) 124 mg

Lamb And Chickpea Stew

Prep time: 5 min

Cook time: 45 min

Servings: 8

Ingredients:

- 1 tbsp. cooking oil
- 2 lbs. cubed lamb shoulder
- 2 chopped white onions
- 4 chopped garlic cloves.
- 28 oz. diced tomatoes
- ¾ cup low-salt chicken broth
- 1 cinnamon stick
- ½ cup dried chickpeas
- 1 tbsp. ground coriander

- 1 tbsp. ground cumin
- 1 tsp. black pepper
- ½ tsp. cayenne pepper
- ¼ tsp. ground cloves
- ¼ tsp. sea salt

To Serve:

- Fresh cilantro
- Plain yogurt

Preparation:

1. Mix together the coriander, cumin, cayenne pepper, cloves, black pepper, and salt in a medium bowl.
2. Add the lamb and toss well to coat.
3. Select the "Sauté" function on the Instant Pot, add the oil and warm up the pot.
4. Sauté the onions and garlic about 5 minutes until softened, and then push aside the onions and return the lamb, sautéing until browned.
5. Stir in the broth, tomatoes, cinnamon, and chickpeas.
6. Close and seal the Instant Pot lid.
7. Set the pressure release valve to "Sealing", and then press the "Cancel" button to stop the "Sauté" function.
8. Select the "Manual, High Pressure" setting and cook for 45 minutes.
9. Once the cook cycle is up, press the "Cancel" button and allow the pressure to release naturally, about 30 minutes.
10. Remove the lid, discard the cinnamon and then taste and adjust the seasonings.
11. Serve garnished with fresh cilantro and yogurt for garnish.
12. This flavorful lamb will keep for up to 4 days refrigerated.

Nutritional information:

Calories 240, Carbs 15g, Fat 10 g, Protein 24g, Potassium (K) 685.9 mg, Sodium (Na) 300 mg

Lamb Curry

Prep time: 10 min

Cook time: 20 min

Servings: 4

Ingredients:

- 2 lbs. diced lamb shoulder
- 2 chopped onions
- 5 minced garlic cloves
- 1 chopped bell pepper
- 4 chopped carrots
- 15 oz. diced tomatoes
- 1 cup coconut milk
- ¼ cup water
- ¼ cup lemon juice
- 6 oz. fresh baby spinach
- 1½ tbsps. curry powder
- 1 tsp. ground ginger
- ½ tsp. kosher salt
- ¼ tsp. black pepper
- ¼ tsp. cayenne pepper

Preparation:

1. Press the "Sauté" function on your Instant Pot and sear the lamb on all sides. Set side.
2. Discard the rendered fat, leaving 1 tablespoon in the Instant Pot.
3. Add the vegetables and cook for about 5-7 minutes until softened.
4. Add in the garlic, ginger, curry powder, salt, black pepper, and cayenne pepper (if using). Stir until all the spices have bloomed.
5. Return the seared lamb to the pot, and stir well to coat completely in the sautéed vegetables and spices.
6. Pour in the tomatoes along with their juices. Stir.
7. Add the coconut milk, with ¼ cup water, and gently stir.
8. Cover, setting the pressure release valve to "Sealing", and cook on "Manual, High Pressure" for 20 minutes.
9. Once done, release the pressure naturally for 10 minutes and then release any remaining pressure.
10. Add the baby spinach and let it cook in the residual heat for about 5-10 minutes, stirring well.
11. Stir in the lemon juice, and serve garnished with cilantro or mint.

Nutritional information:

Calories 273, Carbs 17g, Fat 13 g, Protein 22g, Potassium (K) 936 mg, Sodium (Na) 326 mg

Beef Pot Roast

Prep time: 30 min

Cook time: 45 min

Servings: 5

Ingredients:

- 3 tsp. extra-virgin olive oil, divided
- 2 lbs. beef chuck roast
- 4 quartered red potatoes
- 4 sliced carrots
- 2 quartered yellow onions
- 2 dried bay leaves
- 2 cups low-sodium beef broth
- 2 tbsps. Worcestershire sauce
- 1 tbsp. cider vinegar
- 1 tbsp. cornstarch
- 1 tbsp. tomato paste
- 1 tbsp. minced garlic
- 1 tbsp. smoked paprika
- 1 tsp. black pepper
- ½ tsp. kosher salt
- ¼ tsp. cayenne pepper

Preparation:

1. Select the "Sauté" function on your Instant Pot and heat 2 teaspoons of oil.
2. Add the meat and sear on all sides, about 3 minutes per side. Set aside for now.
3. Add the remaining teaspoon of oil to the pot.
4. Add the bay leaves, tomato paste, garlic, black pepper, paprika, salt and cayenne pepper to the pot, and stir cooking for 1 minute.
5. Stir in the broth and Worcestershire sauce, deglazing the pot. Add the potatoes and carrots.
6. Place the roast on top of the vegetables, and scatter the onions on top.
7. Close and seal the lid, setting the pressure release valve to "Sealing."
8. Cook on "Manual, High Pressure" setting for 45 minutes.
9. Once done, release the pressure manually and uncover the beef.
10. Transfer the beef and vegetables to a platter and gently shred the meat.
11. Skim the fat off the cooking liquid in the pot.
12. Transfer ¼ cup of the cooking juices to a small bowl and set aside.
13. Return the pot to the "Sauté" function and bring the remaining liquid to a simmer.
14. Whisk the cornstarch and reserved ¼ cup of liquid, and then add to the pot.
15. Simmer until the sauce thickens, about 5 to 8 minutes, and then stir in the vinegar.
16. Serve the sauce over the shredded beef and vegetables.

Nutritional information:

Calories 296, Carbs 24g, Fat 8 g, Protein 29g, Potassium (K) 878 mg, Sodium (Na) 508 mg

Mustard Pork Chops

Prep time: 10 minutes

Cook time: 25 minutes

Servings: 4

Ingredients:

- 4 pork chops
- 2 tsps. salt
- 1 tbsp. ground black pepper
- 2 tbsps. honey
- 15 oz. mustard barbecue sauce
- 1 cup water

Preparation:

1. Plugin instant pot, insert the inner pot, add honey, barbecue sauce and water and whisk until mixed.
2. Season pork chops with salt and black pepper, then add to the instant pot, shut the instant pot with its lid and turn the pressure knob to seal the pot.
3. Press the 'manual' button, then press the 'timer' to set the cooking time to 15 minutes and cook at high pressure, instant pot will take 5 minutes or more for building its inner pressure.
4. When the timer beeps, press 'cancel' button and do quick pressure release until pressure nob drops down.
5. Open the instant pot, press the 'sauté/simmer' button and cook for 5 minutes or until cooking sauce in instant pot is reduce by half.
6. Press the cancel button, transfer pork chops to serving plates and ladle cooking sauce over it.
7. Serve straight away.

Nutritional information:

Calories 165, Carbs 9g, Fat 5 g, Protein 19g, Potassium (K) 320 mg, Sodium (Na) 228.7 mg

Pork Roast

Prep time: 15 minutes
Cook time: 50 minutes
Servings: 6

Ingredients:

- 2 lbs. pork roast
- 1 tsp. garlic powder
- 2 tsps. salt
- ½ tsp. ground black pepper
- 1 tsp. dried thyme
- 1 tsp. dried rosemary
- 1 tbsp. oil
- 2 cups chicken broth

Preparation:

1. Stir together garlic, salt, black pepper, thyme, and rosemary and sprinkle this mixture on all sides of pork or until evenly coated.
2. Plugin instant pot, insert the inner pot, press the 'sauté/simmer' button, add 1 tablespoon oil and when hot, add seasoned pork and cook for 4 minutes per side.
3. When done, transfer pork to a plate, then pour in chicken broth and stir well to remove browned bits from the bottom of the instant pot.
4. Press the cancel button, insert trivet stand, place pork on it, then shut the instant pot with its lid and turn the pressure knob to seal the pot.
5. Press the 'meat/stew' button, then press the 'timer' to set the cooking time to 30 minutes and cook at high pressure, instant pot will take 5 minutes or more for building its inner pressure.
6. When the timer beeps, press 'cancel' button and do natural pressure release for 10 minutes and then do quick pressure release until pressure nob drops down.
7. Open the instant pot, transfer pork to a cutting board and let rest for 10 minutes.
8. Cut pork into even slices and serve.

Nutritional information:

Calories 478, Carbs 9.5g, Fat 18.1 g, Protein 66.1 g, Potassium (K) 280 mg, Sodium (Na) 55 mg

Balsamic Beef Pot Roast

Prep time: 15 minutes

Cook time: 50 minutes

Servings: 3

Ingredients:

- 3 lbs. chuck roast, boneless
- ½ cup chopped white onion
- 1 tsp. garlic powder
- 1 tbsp. salt
- 1 tsp. black ground pepper
- ¼ tsp. xanthan gum
- ¼ cup balsamic vinegar
- 1 tbsp. olive oil
- 2 cups beef broth
- 2 tbsps. chopped parsley

Preparation:

1. Stir together garlic, salt, and black pepper and rub this mixture on all sides of roast until evenly coated.
2. Plugin instant pot, insert the inner pot, press sauté/simmer button, add oil and when hot, add seasoned roast and cook for 4 minutes per side or until nicely golden brown.
3. Add remaining ingredients except for xanthan gum and parsley, stir until mixed and press the cancel button.
4. Shut the instant pot with its lid, turn the pressure knob to seal the pot, press the 'manual' button, then press the 'timer' to set the cooking time to 30 minutes and cook at high pressure, instant pot will take 5 minutes or more for building its inner pressure.
5. When the timer beeps, press 'cancel' button and do natural pressure release for 10 minutes and then do quick pressure release until pressure nob drops down.
6. Open the instant pot, transfer roast to a plate and break into bite-size pieces.
7. Press the 'sauté/simmer' button, add xanthan gum into the instant pot and cook for 3 to 5 minutes or until cooking sauce is reduced by half.
8. Return beef into the instant pot, stir until just mixed and press the cancel button.
9. Garnish beef with parsley and serve.

Nutritional information:

Calories 322, Carbs 94g, Fat20 g, Protein 32 g, Potassium (K) 193 mg, Sodium (Na) 265.2 mg

Beef Stroganoff

Prep time: 20 minutes

Cook time: 60 minutes

Servings: 6

Ingredients:

- 2 lbs. beef steak
- ½ cup flour
- 2 cups sliced mushrooms
- 1 chopped white onion
- 1½ tsp. minced garlic
- ½ tsp. salt
- 1 tbsp. Worcestershire sauce
- ¼ tsp. black pepper
- 3 tbsps. olive oil
- 14 oz. beef broth
- 1 cup sour cream

Preparations:

1. Cut beef into 1-inch pieces and then coat with ¼ cup flour.
2. Plugin instant pot, insert the inner pot, press sauté/simmer button, add oil and when hot, add coated beef pieces in a single layer and cook for 7 to 10 minutes or until nicely browned.
3. Cook remaining beef pieces in the same manner and then transfer to a bowl.
4. Then add onion and garlic and cook for 3 minutes or until sauté.
5. Add mushrooms, season with salt and black pepper, drizzle with Worcestershire sauce, pour in the broth, then return beef pieces and stir until mixed.
6. Press the cancel button, shut the instant pot with its lid and turn the pressure knob to seal the pot.
7. Press the 'manual' button, then press the 'timer' to set the cooking time to 30 minutes and cook at high pressure, instant pot will take 5 minutes or more for building its inner pressure.
8. When the timer beeps, press 'cancel' button and do natural pressure release for 10 minutes and then do quick pressure release until pressure nob drops down.
9. Open the lid, stir beef stroganoff and if the sauce is too thin, press the 'sauté/simmer' button and cook the sauce for 5 minutes or more until sauce is slightly thick.
10. Then press the cancel button, add sour cream into the instant pot and stir until combined.
11. Serve straight away.

Nutritional information:

Calories 382.6, Carbs 13.1g, Fat 17.9 g, Protein 38.2 g, Potassium (K) 496 mg, Sodium (Na) 300 mg

Fish and Seafood

Lemon Pepper And Dill Salmon

Prep time: 5 minutes

Cook time: 5 minutes

Servings: 4

Ingredients:

- 2 tbsp. butter
- 1 lb. salmon filet
- 1 sliced lemon
- 3 thyme sprigs
- 1 fresh dill sprig
- 1 tsp. chopped dill
- Juice of 1 lemon
- Zest of 1 lemon
- 1 tsp. sea salt
- ¼ tsp. black pepper

Preparation:

1. Add the butter, lemon zest, lemon juice, dill, salt, and pepper to a small mixing bowl. Mix well to form a compound butter.
2. Cut salmon into portion sizes, and place dollops of the compound butter all around the salmon portions.
3. Pour a cup of water into the Instant Pot, along with some thyme and/or dill.
4. Place half of the salmon onto a standard trivet and insert this into the pot.
5. Season with more pepper, and then top the fish with 2 thin slices of lemon.
6. Place the second half of the fish onto a 3-inch trivet and insert into the pot. Season with more black pepper, and then top the salmon again with 2 thin slices of lemon.
7. Close and lock the lid, cooking on "Manual, High Pressure" for 3 minutes.
8. Once done, quick release the pressure.
9. Uncover, and serve immediately.

Nutritional information:

Calories 224, Carbs 3g, Fat 13g, Protein 22 g, Potassium (K) 602 mg, Sodium (Na) 581 mg

Rosemary Salmon

Prep time: 5 minutes

Cook time: 15 minutes

Servings: 3

Ingredients:

- 1 tbsp. olive oil
- 1 lb. frozen, wild-caught salmon
- 1 sprig fresh rosemary
- 10 oz. fresh asparagus
- ½ cup halved cherry tomatoes
- 1 tbsp. lemon juice
- 1 tsp. Kosher salt
- Black pepper

Preparation:

1. Pour a cup of water into the Instant Pot and place a wire rack into the pot.
2. Place the fish in a single layer onto the rack, and then add a sprig of rosemary and finally the fresh asparagus.
3. Choose the "Manual, High pressure" setting and adjust the cook time to 3 minutes.
4. Once done, release the pressure and uncover the pot.
5. Remove the lid and transfer all the contents onto a plate, discarding the rosemary.
6. Add the cherry tomatoes, drizzle with olive oil and season with salt and black pepper.
7. Sprinkle with lemon juice and serve.

Nutritional information:

Calories 282, Carbs 5g, Fat 14 g, Protein 32 g, Potassium (K) 985 mg, Sodium (Na) 71 mg

Shrimp With Tomatoes And Feta

Prep time: 10 minutes

Cook time: 12 minutes

Servings: 6

Ingredients:

- 2 tbsp. butter
- 1 lb. frozen shrimp
- 1 tbsp. garlic
- 1½ cups chopped white onion
- 14.5 oz. crushed tomatoes
- 1 tsp. dried oregano
- 1 tsp. sea salt
- ½ tsp. red pepper flakes, or to taste

To Serve:

- 1 cup crumbled feta cheese
- ½ cup sliced black olives
- ¼ cup fresh parsley

Preparation:

1. Select the "Sauté" function on your Instant Pot and once hot, add the butter.
2. Melt the butter and then add the garlic and red pepper flakes.
3. Next, add in the onions, tomatoes, salt, and oregano.
4. Add the frozen shrimp.
5. Set the Instant pot on "Manual, High Pressure" setting for1 minute.

6. Once done, release all the pressure and stir well to combine all the ingredients.
7. Allow to cool and then sprinkle with feta cheese, black olives, and parsley.
8. Serve with buttered French bread, or rice.

Nutritional information:

Calories 211, Carbs 6g, Fat 11 g, Protein 19 g, Potassium (K) 148 mg, Sodium (Na) 1468 mg

Lemon Pepper Salmon

Prep time: 5 minutes

Cook time: 10 minutes

Servings: 4

Ingredients:

- 3 tbsps. ghee or avocado oil
- 1 lb. skin-on salmon filet
- 1 julienned red bell pepper
- 1 julienned green zucchini
- 1 julienned carrot
- ¾ cup water
- A few sprigs of parsley, tarragon, dill, basil or a combination
- ½ sliced lemon
- ½ tsp. black pepper
- ¼ tsp. sea salt

Preparation:

1. Add the water and the herbs into the bottom of the Instant Pot and put in a wire steamer rack making sure the handles extend upwards.
2. Place the salmon filet onto the wire rack, with the skin side facing down.
3. Drizzle the salmon with ghee, season with black pepper and salt, and top with the lemon slices.
4. Close and seal the Instant Pot, making sure the vent is turned to "Sealing".
5. Select the "Steam" setting and cook for 3 minutes.
6. While the salmon cooks, julienne the vegetables, and set aside.
7. Once done, quick release the pressure, and then press the "Keep Warm/Cancel" button.
8. Uncover and wearing oven mitts, carefully remove the steamer rack with the salmon.
9. Remove the herbs and discard them.
10. Add the vegetables to the pot and put the lid back on.
11. Select the "Sauté" function and cook for 1-2 minutes.
12. Serve the vegetables with salmon and add the remaining fat to the pot.
13. Pour a little of the sauce over the fish and vegetables if desired.

Nutritional information:

Calories 296, Carbs 8g, Fat 15 g, Protein 31 g, Potassium (K) 1084 mg, Sodium (Na) 284 mg

Coconut Shrimp Curry

Prep time: 5 minutes

Cook time: 15 minutes

Servings: 4

Ingredients:

- 1 tbsp. vegetable oil
- 1 lb. frozen shrimp
- 1 cup chopped white onion
- ½ tbsp. minced ginger
- ½ tbsp. minced garlic
- 1 tsp. mustard seeds
- 1 green chili pepper
- 1 cup chopped tomato
- ¼ can coconut milk

- 1 tbsp. lime juice
- ¼ cup cilantro

For the Spice mix:

- 1 tsp. coriander powder
- ½ tsp. cayenne or red chili powder
- ½ tsp. ground turmeric
- ½ tsp. garam masala
- ½ tsp. sea salt

Preparations:

1. Select the "Sauté" function on the instant Pot and allow it to heat up.
2. Add the oil and mustard seeds and sizzle them until they begin to pop.
3. Add the onions, ginger, garlic and green chili.
4. Sauté for 5 minutes until the onions are a light golden brown and the garlic and ginger aromatic.
5. Add the tomato and all the spices. Mix and sauté for 2-3 minutes.
6. Now, add the coconut milk and shrimp. Stir and select the "Cancel" button. Close the lid with steam release vent in the "Sealing" position.
7. Cook on the "Manual, Low Pressure" setting for 3 minutes.
8. Once done, quick release the pressure manually.
9. Stir in the lime and garnish with cilantro.
10. Enjoy and serve with rice.

Nutritional information:

Calories 226, Carbs 8g, Fat 10 g, Protein 24 g, Potassium (K) 289 mg, Sodium (Na) 1222 mg

Trout Bake

Prep time: 15 minutes

Cook time: 35 minutes

Servings: 2

Ingredients:

- 1 lb. trout fillets
- 1 lb. chopped winter vegetables
- 1 cup low sodium fish broth
- 1 tbsp. mixed herbs
- 1 tsp. Salt

Preparation:

1. Mix all the ingredients except the broth in a foil pouch.
2. Place the pouch in the steamer basket your Instant Pot.
3. Pour the broth into the Instant Pot.
4. Cook on Steam for 35 minutes.
5. Release the pressure naturally.

Nutritional information:

Calories 310, Carbs 14g, Fat 12 g, Protein 40 g, Potassium (K) 335 mg, Sodium (Na) 229 mg

Tuna Sweetcorn Casserole

Prep time: 15 minutes

Cook time: 35 minutes

Servings: 2

Ingredients:

- 3 small tins of tuna
- ½ lb. sweetcorn kernels
- 1 lb. chopped vegetables
- 1 cup low sodium vegetable broth
- 2 tbsps. spicy seasoning

Preparation:

1. Mix all the ingredients in your Instant Pot.
2. Cook on Stew for 35 minutes.
3. Release the pressure naturally.

Nutritional information:

Calories 226, Carbs 8g, Fat 10 g, Protein 24 g, Potassium (K) 571.2 mg, Sodium (Na) 176 mg

Swordfish Steak

Prep time: 15 minutes

Cooking time: 35 minutes

Setting: Steam

Serves: 2

Ingredients:

- 1 lb. swordfish steak
- 1 lb. chopped Mediterranean vegetables
- 1 cup low sodium fish broth
- 2 tbsps. soy sauce

Preparation:

1. Mix all the ingredients except the broth in a foil pouch.
2. Place the pouch in the steamer basket for your Instant Pot.
3. Pour the broth into the Instant Pot. Lower the steamer basket into the Instant Pot.
4. Cook on Steam for 35 minutes.
5. Release the pressure naturally.

Nutritional information:

Calories 270, Carbs 5g, Fat 10 g, Protein 48 g, Potassium (K) 391.1 mg, Sodium (Na) 100 mg

Mussels And Spaghetti Squash

Prep time: 15 minutes

Cook time: 35 minutes

Servings: 2

Ingredients:

- 1lb cooked, shelled mussels
- 1/2 a spaghetti squash, to fit the Instant Pot
- 1 cup low sodium fish broth
- 3tbsp crushed garlic
- sea salt to taste

Preparation:

1. Mix the mussels with the garlic and salt. Place the mussels inside the squash.
2. Lower the squash into your Instant Pot.
3. Pour the broth around it, cook on Stew for 35 minutes.
4. Release the pressure naturally.
5. Shred the squash, mixing the "spaghetti" with the mussels.

Nutritional information:

Calories 265, Carbs 7g, Fat 9 g, Protein 24 g, Potassium (K) 124.8 mg, Sodium (Na) 462.6 mg

Cod In White Sauce

Prep time: 15 minutes

Cook time: 5 minutes

Servings: 2

Ingredients:

- 1 lb. cod fillets
- 1 lb. chopped swede and carrots
- 2 cups white sauce
- 1 cup peas
- 3 tbsps. black pepper

Preparation:

1. Mix all the ingredients in your Instant Pot, cook on Stew for 5 minutes.
2. Release the pressure naturally and serve.

Nutritional information:

Calories 390, Carbs 10g, Fat 26 g, Protein 41 g, Potassium (K) 510.4 mg, Sodium (Na) 207.5 mg

Poultry

Buffalo Chicken Chili

Prep time: 10 minutes

Cook time: 30 minutes

Servings: 8

Ingredients:

- 2 lbs. skinless and boneless chicken breasts
- 1 chopped white onion
- 5 minced garlic cloves
- 3 chopped carrots
- 3 chopped celery stalks
- 28 oz. diced tomatoes
- 15 oz. low-sodium beans
- ¼ cup Frank's red hot sauce
- 2 tbsps. maple syrup or honey
- 1 tbsp. chili powder
- 1 tbsp. ground cumin
- 1 tbsp. smoked paprika
- ½ tsp. salt
- ½ crumbled blue cheese

Preparations:

1. In your Instant Pot, add all the ingredients, staring with the garlic, onion, carrots, celery, beans, maple syrup, ground cumin, chili powder, smoked paprika, salt, chicken, hot sauce and finish with the canned diced tomatoes. Do not stir the mixture.
2. Close and seal the lid, and set the steam release vent to "Scaling" and choose to cook on the "Manual, High Pressure" setting for 30 minutes.
3. Once cooked, release the pressure, by performing a quick pressure release. Turn the steam release valve to the "Venting" position until the dial completely drops down.
4. Remove the chicken breasts, shred, and return to the Instant Pot.
5. Add blue cheese, stir and rest for a few minutes.
6. Serve hot, garnished with green onion, cilantro, and lime.

Nutritional information:

Calories 313, Carbs 29.2g, Fat 6 g, Protein 35.1 g, Potassium (K) 674.5 mg, Sodium (Na) 728.2 mg

Butter Chicken

Prep time: 10 min

Cook time: 25 min

Servings: 8

Ingredients:

- 3.5 lbs. chicken drumsticks or thighs
- 1 chopped white onion
- 4 minced garlic cloves
- 2 minced ginger root
- 2 cups water
- 14 oz. full-fat coconut milk
- 6 oz. tomato paste
- 2 tbsps. maple syrup
- ¼ cup cold water
- 4 tbsps. cornstarch

- 1 tbsp. garam masala
- 1 tbsp. curry powder
- 1 tsp. chili powder
- 1¼ tsps. salt
- ½ tsp. black pepper

To Garnish:

- Cilantro
- Green onion

To Serve:

- Brown rice

Preparation:

1. Add all the ingredients for the curry starting with the water, onion, garlic, ginger, curry powder, garam masala, chili powder, salt, pepper, coconut milk, tomato paste, maple syrup, and finally the chicken.
2. Close and seal the lid, setting the pressure vent to "Sealing" and cook on "Manual, High Pressure" for 20 minutes. It will take the pot about 15 minutes to come to pressure.
3. After 20 minutes, the Instant Pot will beep, to indicate it is done with the cooking.
4. Allow for a natural pressure release, about 20 minutes, or if you're in a hurry, you can do a quick pressure release by turning the pressure release valve to the "Venting" position, about 2-3 minutes.
5. Carefully open the lid and choose the "Sauté" function.
6. Whisk together the cornstarch and water to form a slurry and pour over the chicken. Stir gently.
7. Cook until the sauce has thickened, and serve with brown rice, topped with cilantro and green onions.

Nutritional information:

Calories 385, Carbs 14g, Fat 17.6 g, Protein 39.2 g, Potassium (K) 725.5 mg, Sodium (Na) 553.2 mg

Instant Pot Chicken Breast

Prep time: 2 minutes

Cook time: 20 minutes

Servings: 8

Ingredients:

- 3 lbs. boneless and skinless chicken breasts
- 1 cup water
- 2 tsp. garlic powder
- Black pepper
- 1 tsp. salt

Preparations:

1. Pour in water into the Instant Pot and place a trivet with handles inside.
2. Place the chicken breasts into the Instant Pot, arranging them in a single layer.
3. If using frozen chicken make sure each breast is separated, and not touching each other.
4. Season with garlic powder, black pepper, and salt, toss well to mix using tongs or your hands.
5. Close and seal the lid, setting the pressure release vent to "Sealing" and choose the "Manual, High Pressure" setting.
6. Cook for 20 minutes if using fresh chicken or 25 minutes if using frozen chicken breasts.
7. The Instant Pot will take 10 minutes to come to pressure, so factor this time in your cooking.
8. After the cook cycle is done, the Instant Pot will beep, and will need about 20 minutes to come down to pressure. This is known as a Natural Pressure Release, and should take about 10-15 minutes.
9. A quick release will not work for this recipe, as it makes the meat tough.
10. Carefully open the lid and use the chicken breasts for meal prep, casseroles, salads etc.
11. Shred or cube the chicken, and save the stock for other recipes like soup.

Nutritional information:

Calories 204, Carbs 0 g, Fat 4.5 g, Protein 38.3 g, Potassium (K) 496 mg, Sodium (Na) 294.5 mg

Moroccan Chicken Bowls

Prep time: 20 minutes

Cook time: 25 minutes

Servings: 6

Ingredients:

For the Sweet Potatoes:
- 2 cubed sweet potatoes
- ½ tbsp. olive oil
- 1 tsp. garlic powder
- ½ tbsp. chili powder

For the chicken:
- 3 tbsp. olive oil
- 1½ lbs. chicken thighs
- 1 chopped white onion
- ⅓ cup raisins
- ½ cup chopped green olives
- ½ cup chicken broth
- 1 tbsp. ground cumin
- ½ tbsp. chili powder
- 1 tsp. ginger powder
- 1 tsp. turmeric
- 1½ tsp. garlic powder
- ½ tsp. cayenne
- ⅛ tsp. salt

For the Couscous:
- 1 cup water
- 1 cup couscous
- Zest of 1 lemon
- 2 tbsp. lemon juice
- ¼ cup chopped cilantro
- ¼ cup chopped parsley

To Serve:
- Feta cheese
- Pistachios

Preparation:
1. Preheat the oven to 400F.
2. Prepare a baking sheet and then put the sweet potatoes onto the baking sheet.
3. Drizzle the potatoes with olive oil, chili powder, and garlic powder, and mix.
4. Bake for 20-25 minutes.
5. Prepare the marinade for the chicken by mixing together the turmeric, cumin, ginger, chili powder, garlic powder, cayenne, and salt.
6. Place the chicken thighs into a bowl and pour over the spices. Rub, making sure each thigh is well coated, and set aside.
7. Select the "Sauté" function on the Instant Pot and then add two tablespoons of olive oil.
8. Once hot, place the chicken thighs with the skin side facing down, and cook for 2-3 minutes.
9. Flip over and cook for 2-3 minutes more, before removing from the Instant Pot.

10. Add all the remaining ingredients for the chicken to the pot, place the chicken on top, and then close and seal your Instant Pot.
11. Set the Instant Pot on the "Manual, High Pressure" setting and once the pot is up to pressure, cook for 25 minutes.
12. As the chicken cooks, prepare the couscous.
13. Bring 2 cups of water to a boil.
14. Place the couscous in a bowl, and add the boiling water to it.
15. Cover with cling wrap, and let rest for 5 minutes. After 5 minutes, uncover the couscous and fluff with a fork.
16. In another large mixing bowl, combine the ingredients for the couscous, and set them aside.
17. When the chicken is done, the naturally release the pressure, about 5-10 minutes.
18. Carefully uncover and remove the chicken from Instant pot and then shred into bits.
19. Discard the skin and bones and return the shredded chicken to the Instant Pot, and mix well with the cooking juices.
20. Serve the chicken with sweet potatoes and couscous, and if desired, top with feta cheese and pistachios.

Nutritional information:

Calories 346, Carbs 30g, Fat 15 g, Protein 26 g, Potassium (K) 941.9 mg, Sodium (Na) 239.9 mg

Lemon Chicken With Garlic

Prep time: 8 minutes

Cook time: 20 minutes

Servings: 8

Ingredients:

- 2 tbsps. olive oil
- 3 tbsps. butter
- 8 skinless, boneless chicken thighs
- ½ chopped white onion
- 4 minced garlic cloves
- ⅓ cup low-sodium chicken broth
- 2 tbsps. heavy cream
- 4 tsps. Italian seasoning
- ½ tsp. smoked paprika
- ½ tsp. garlic powder
- ½ tsp. red chili flakes optional or to taste
- Zest of ½ a lemon
- Juice of 1 lemon
- Coarse sea salt
- Black pepper

To Garnish:

- Lemon slices
- Chopped parsley

Preparation:

1. Season the skin and cavity of the chicken with paprika, garlic powder, sea salt, black pepper, garlic powder, and chili flakes.
2. Select the "Sauté" function on Normal on your Instant Pot.
3. Add olive oil to the inner pot of a large 6-quart Instant Pot and allow it to get hot.
4. Place the seasoned chicken into the Instant Pot and cook for 2-3 minutes per side, until golden brown.
5. Once the chicken is light and golden brown, remove the chicken from Instant Pot and set it aside.
6. Melt the butter, and stir in the chopped onions and minced garlic.
7. Deglaze the pot with lemon juice, and cook for 1 minute.
8. Now add the Italian seasoning, chicken broth, and lemon zest.
9. Return the chicken into the Instant Pot, and then close and seal the lid, turning the steam release valve to "Sealing."
10. Select the "Manual, High Pressure" setting on older models or the "Pressure Cook" setting on newer models, and cook for 7 minutes. Note that the Instant Pot will take 5-10 minutes to come up to pressure.
11. Once done, quick release the pressure after 2 minutes, and then uncover the pot.
12. Remove the chicken using tongs and then it set aside.
13. Take the heavy cream and stir it into the Instant Pot.
14. You may also add a cornstarch, arrowroot starch slurry, or xanthan gum, by mixing ½ a teaspoon cornstarch or arrowroot starch) mixed with 1 teaspoon of cold water.
15. Press the "Off" button, turning the Instant Pot to the "Sauté" function.

16. Allow the sauce to thicken, and then turn off the pot and add the chicken back into the pot.
17. Spoon the cooking juices all over the chicken and garnish with chopped parsley.
18. Serve with creamed mashed cauliflower, and garnish with lemon slices, if desired.

Nutritional information:

Calories 282, Carbs 2g, Fat 15 g, Protein 14 g, Potassium (K) 317.0 mg, Sodium (Na) 416 mg

Cilantro Lime Chicken

Prep time: 3 minutes

Cook time: 15 minutes

Servings: 6

Ingredients:

- 2 lbs. boneless and skinless chicken breasts
- 1 chopped jalapeño
- 24 oz. no-sugar salsa
- 14 oz. low-sodium black beans
- 1 packet low-sodium taco seasoning
- ¼ cup water or low-sodium chicken stock
- Juice and zest of 1 lime

To Garnish:

- Chopped cilantro

Preparation:

1. Take a 6-quart or larger Instant Pot and add to it all the ingredients for the chicken, except the fresh cilantro.
2. Close and seal the lid, making sure the pressure valve is set to "Sealing", and then cook on "Manual, High Pressure" for 15 minutes.
3. Once the cook cycle is up, allow for a natural pressure release for 10 minutes, followed by a quick release of any remaining pressure.
4. Uncover, and using two forks, shred the chicken breast.
5. Add the chopped cilantro and then stir everything well to incorporate all the ingredients.
6. Serve, top with your favorite toppings, and enjoy!

Nutritional information:

Calories 272, Carbs 27g, Fat 4 g, Protein 33 g, Potassium (K) 188.5 mg, Sodium (Na) 102.5 mg

Chicken Tikka Masala

Prep time: 10 minutes

Cook time: 50 minutes

Servings: 6

Ingredients:

- 2 lbs. diced chicken breasts
- 1 tbsp. unsalted butter
- 1 chopped yellow onion
- 3 minced garlic cloves
- 1 tbsp. minced ginger
- 14 oz. light coconut milk
- 8 oz. no-sodium tomato sauce
- ¾ cup frozen peas
- ½ cup plain non-fat Greek yogurt

- 1 tbsp. garam masala
- 1½ tsp. kosher salt
- 1 tsp. ground chili powder
- 1 tsp. ground turmeric
- 1 tsp. ground cumin
- ¼ tsp. ground cayenne, or to taste

To Serve:

- Chopped cilantro
- Prepared brown rice

Preparation:

1. Season the chicken with kosher salt and set it aside.
2. Add butter to the Instant Pot and select the "Sauté" function.
3. Once the butter has melted, add in the chopped onion, ginger, garlic, ginger, chili powder, garam masala, cayenne, cumin, and turmeric.
4. Sauté until the onion is softened and the spices have bloomed, about 5 minutes.
5. Add the chicken, and stir to coat until the outsides of the chicken begin to brown, about 4 minutes.
6. Add the tomato sauce and the reserved ½ a teaspoon of salt. Stir well.
7. Cover and seal the lid, making sure the pressure valve is set to "Sealing."
8. Cook on "Manual, High Pressure" for 8 minutes, and then once cooked, vent to immediately release any remaining pressure.
9. Uncover, stir in the coconut milk, and turn the Instant Pot back to the "Sauté" function.
10. Simmer for about 10-15 minutes, until the sauce slightly thickens.
11. Turn the Instant Pot off.
12. Site in the peas, cool for 3-4 minutes, and stir in the Greek yogurt.
13. Enjoy warm with naan bread or rice, and a garnish with fresh cilantro.

Nutritional information:

Calories 355, Carbs 32g, Fat 10 g, Protein 36 g, Potassium (K) 748 mg, Sodium (Na) 654 mg

Chicken Piccata

Prep time: 10 minutes

Cook time: 20 minutes

Servings: 3

Ingredients:

- 1 tbsp. extra-virgin olive oil
- 2 lbs. boneless, skinless chicken breasts
- 1 minced garlic cloves
- 4 oz. drained capers
- ¾ cup low-sodium chicken stock
- ¼ cup squeezed lemon juice
- 1 tsp. dried basil
- 1 tsp. dried oregano
- Kosher salt
- Black pepper

Preparation:

1. Select the "Sauté" function on your Instant and add oil.
2. Season the chicken and add to the hot Instant Pot.
3. Brown for about 4 minutes per side and then set aside on a plate.
4. Add the minced garlic and sauté, cooking for about 1 minute, until fragrant.
5. Next, add the lemon juice, broth, basil, and oregano, and deglaze the bottom of the Instant Pot.
6. Return the seared chicken to Instant Pot and sprinkle with capers.
7. Cover and seal the Instant Pot, making sure the pressure valve is set to "Sealing."
8. Cook on the "Manual, High Pressure" setting for 10 minutes.
9. Once done, do a quick pressure release and uncover the pot.
10. Use an instant read meat thermometer; the internal temperature of the chicken should read 165F.
11. Serve immediately with your favorite side.

Nutritional information:

Calories 239, Carbs 4g, Fat 8 g, Protein 42 g, Potassium (K) 370 mg, Sodium (Na) 928 mg

Turkey Burger Patty

Prep time: 5 minutes

Cook time: 20 minutes

Servings: 6

Ingredients:

- 2 lbs. ground turkey
- 2 tsps. salt
- 1 tsp. ground black pepper
- 1 tsp. red chili powder
- ¾ tsp. cumin
- 1 cup water

Preparation:

1. Place ground turkey in a large bowl, season with salt, black pepper, red chili powder and cumin and then shape mixture into six patties.
2. Plugin instant pot, insert the inner pot, pour in water, and then insert a steamer basket.
3. Wrap each patty with aluminum foil, place them on the steamer basket, then shut the instant pot with its lid and turn the pressure knob to seal the pot.
4. Press the 'manual' button, then press the 'timer' to set the cooking time to 15 minutes and cook at high pressure, instant pot will take 5 minutes or more for building its inner pressure.
5. When the timer beeps, press 'cancel' button and do quick pressure release until pressure nob drops down.
6. Open the instant pot, remove and uncover patties and serve.

Nutritional information:

Calories 212, Carbs 0g, Fat 14g, Protein 22 g, Potassium (K) 206 mg, Sodium (Na) 69 mg

Spinach Stuffed Chicken Breast

Prep time: 15 minutes

Cook time: 20 minutes

Servings: 4

Ingredients:

- 4 chicken breasts
- 4 chopped artichoke heart
- 4 tsps. chopped sundried tomato
- 2 tsps. minced garlic
- ¼ sp. ground black pepper
- 1 sp. curry powder
- 1 tsp. paprika
- 20 chopped basil leaves
- 4 oz. chopped low-fat mozzarella cheese
- 1 cup water

Preparation:

1. Place artichoke heart in a bowl, add tomato, garlic, basil, and mozzarella cheese and stir until mixed.
2. Cut each chicken breast halfway through and then season chicken with salt, black pepper, curry powder, and paprika.
3. Stuff chicken with artichoke mixture and close the filling with chicken using a toothpick.
4. Plugin instant pot, insert the inner pot, pour in water, then insert steamer basket and place stuffed chicken breasts on it.
5. Shut the instant pot with its lid, turn the pressure knob to seal the pot, press the 'manual' button, then press the 'timer' to set the cooking time to 15 minutes and cook at high pressure, instant pot will take 5 minutes or more for building its inner pressure.
6. When the timer beeps, press 'cancel' button and do natural pressure release for 10 minutes and then do quick pressure release until pressure nob drops down.
7. Open the instant pot, transfer stuffed chicken to plates and serve.

Nutritional information:

Calories 262, Carbs 8.5g, Fat 4.1g, Protein 46.1 g, Potassium (K) 404.7 mg, Sodium (Na) 953.7 mg

Appetizers and Snacks

Brussels Sprouts

Prep time: 5 minutes

Cook time: 3 minutes

Servings: 5

Ingredients:

- 1 tsp. extra-virgin olive oil
- 1 lb. halved Brussels sprouts
- 3 tbsps. apple cider vinegar
- 3 tbsps. gluten-free tamari soy sauce
- 3 tbsps. chopped sun-dried tomatoes

Preparation:

1. Select the "Sauté" function on your Instant Pot, add oil and allow the pot to get hot.
2. Cancel the "Sauté" function and add the Brussels sprouts.
3. Stir well and allow the sprouts to cook in the residual heat for 2-3 minutes.
4. Add the tamari soy sauce and vinegar, and then stir.
5. Cover the Instant Pot, sealing the pressure valve by pointing it to "Sealing."
6. Select the "Manual, High Pressure" setting and cook for 3 minutes.
7. Once the cook cycle is done, do a quick pressure release, and then stir in the chopped sun dried tomatoes.
8. Serve immediately.

Nutritional information:

Calories 62, Carbs 10g, Fat 1 g, Protein 4 g, Potassium (K) 475 mg, Sodium (Na) 633 mg

Garlic and Herb Carrots

Prep time: 2 minutes

Cook time: 18 minutes

Servings: 3

Ingredients:

- 2 tbsps. butter
- 1 lb. baby carrots
- 1 cup water
- 1 tsp. fresh thyme or oregano
- 1 tsp. minced garlic
- Black pepper
- Coarse sea salt

Preparation:

1. Add water to the inner pot of the Instant Pot, and then put in a steamer basket.
2. Layer the carrots into the steamer basket.
3. Close and seal the lid, with the pressure vent in the "Sealing" position.
4. Select the "Steam" setting and cook for 2 minutes on high pressure.

5. Quick release the pressure and then carefully remove the steamer basket with the steamed carrots, discarding the water.
6. Add butter to the inner pot of the Instant Pot and allow it to melt on the "Sauté" function.
7. Add garlic and sauté for 30 seconds, and then add the carrots. Mix well.
8. Stir in the fresh herbs, and cook for 2-3 minutes.
9. Season with salt and black pepper, and the transfer to a serving bowl.
10. Serve warm and enjoy!

Nutritional information:

Calories 122, Carbs 12g, Fat 7 g, Protein 1 g, Potassium (K) 358 mg, Sodium (Na) 189 mg

Cilantro Lime Drumsticks

Prep time: 5 minutes

Cook time: 15 minutes

Servings: 6

Ingredients:

- 1 tbsp. olive oil
- 6 chicken drumsticks
- 4 minced garlic cloves
- ½ cup low-sodium chicken broth
- 1 tsp. cayenne pepper
- 1 tsp. crushed red peppers
- 1 tsp. fine sea salt
- Juice of 1 lime

To Serve:

- 2 tbsp. chopped cilantro
- Extra lime zest

Preparation:

1. Add olive oil to the Instant Pot and set it on the "Sauté" function.
2. Once the oil is hot add the chicken drumsticks, and season them well.
3. Using tongs, stir the drumsticks and brown the drumsticks for 2 minutes per side.
4. Add the lime juice, fresh cilantro, and chicken broth to the pot.
5. Lock and seal the lid, turning the pressure valve to "Sealing."
6. Cook the drumsticks on the "Manual, High Pressure" setting for 9 minutes.
7. Once done allow the pressure to release naturally.
8. Carefully transfer the drumsticks to an aluminum-foiled baking sheet and broil them in the oven for 3-5 minutes until golden brown.
9. Serve warm, garnished with more cilantro and lime zest.

Nutritional information:

Calories 480, Carbs 3.3g, Fat 29 g, Protein 47.2 g, Potassium (K) 677 mg, Sodium (Na) 1180 mg

Eggplant Spread

Prep time: 5 minutes

Cook time: 18 minutes

Servings: 5

Ingredients:

- 4 tbsps. extra-virgin olive oil
- 2 lbs. eggplant
- 4 skin-on garlic cloves
- ½ cup water
- ¼ cup pitted black olives

- 3 sprigs fresh thyme
- Juice of 1 lemon
- 1 tbsp. tahini
- 1 tsp. sea salt
- Fresh extra-virgin olive oil

Preparation:

1. Peel the eggplant in alternating stripes, leaving some areas with skin and some with no skin.
2. Slice into big chunks and layer at the bottom of your Instant Pot.
3. Add olive oil to the pot, and on the "Sauté" function, fry and caramelize the eggplant on one side, about 5 minutes.
4. Add in the garlic cloves with the skin on.
5. Flip over the eggplant and then add in the remaining uncooked eggplant chunks, salt, and water.
6. Close and seal the lid, making sure the pressure release valve is set to "Sealing."
7. Cook for 5 minutes on the "Manual, High Pressure" setting.
8. Once done, carefully open the pot by quick releasing the pressure through the steam valve.
9. Discard most of the brown cooking liquid.
10. Remove the garlic cloves and peel them.
11. Add the lemon juice, tahini, cooked and fresh garlic cloves and pitted black olives to the pot.
12. Using a hand-held immersion blender, puree all the ingredients until smooth.
13. Pour out the spread into a serving dish and season with fresh thyme, whole black olives and some extra-virgin olive oil, prior to serving.

Nutritional information:

Calories 155.5, Carbs 16.8g, Fat 11.7 g, Protein 2 g, Potassium (K) 170.9 mg, Sodium (Na) 820.9 mg

Cauliflower Mash

Prep time: 5 minutes, Cook time: 8 minutes

Servings: 4

Ingredients:

- ½ tbsps. butter
- 1 large crown cauliflower
- 4 slices low-sodium cooked bacon
- 1½ cups water or chicken broth
- 1 clove garlic
- 1 tbsp. sour cream
- ¼ tsp. dry mustard powder
- ¼ tsp. chili powder
- ¾ cup grated non-fat Cheddar cheese
- ¼ cup grated Parmesan cheese
- Coarse sea salt
- Black pepper

To Serve:

- 2 sliced green onions

Preparation:

1. Preheat your oven to 375F, and then place a wire steamer rack inside your Instant Pot.
2. Transfer the chopped cauliflower to the steamer basket into the Instant Pot.
3. Close and seal the lid and make sure to set the valve to "Sealing."
4. Choose the "Manual, High Pressure" setting and cook for 3 minutes.
5. Once the cook cycle is up, do a quick pressure release, and then drain the cauliflower, placing it into the bowl of a food processor.
6. Add the butter, garlic, sour cream, chili powder, dry mustard, salt, and black pepper to the blender
7. Pulse until smooth and creamy, and then transfer the cauliflower mash to an oven-proof baking dish.
8. Top with both cheeses and the crumbled bacon, and bake for 5 minutes, until the cheese is melted.
9. Garnish with green onions and serve.

Nutritional information:

Calories 235, Carbs 1g, Fat 19g, Protein 12 g, Potassium (K) 101 mg, Sodium (Na) 486 mg

Carrot Hummus

Prep time: 15 minutes

Cooking time: 10 minutes

Servings: 2

Ingredients:

- 1 chopped carrot
- 2 oz. cooked chickpeas
- 1 tsp. lemon juice
- 1 tsp. tahini
- 1 tsp. fresh parsley

Preparation:

1. Place the carrot and chickpeas in your Instant Pot.

2. Add a cup of water, seal, cook for 10 minutes on Stew.
3. Depressurize naturally. Blend with the remaining ingredients.

Nutritional information:

Calories 58, Carbs 8g, Fat 2g, Protein 2 g, Potassium (K) 344 mg, Sodium (Na) 638 mg

Mushroom Tofu Scramble

Prep time: 15 minutes

Cook time: 7 minutes

Servings: 2

Ingredients:

- 1 cup firm tofu
- 1 cup chopped mixed mushrooms
- 3 tbsps. mushroom soup
- 1 tsp. mixed herbs
- 1 tsp. salt

Preparation:

1. Spray a heat-proof bowl that fits in your Instant Pot with nonstick spray.
2. Chop the tofu finely.
3. Mix with the other ingredients. Pour into the bowl.
4. Place the bowl in your steamer basket.
5. Pour 1 cup of water into your Instant Pot. Lower the basket into your Instant Pot.
6. Seal and cook on low pressure for 7 minutes. Depressurize quickly.
7. Stir well and allow to rest, it will finish cooking in its own heat.

Nutritional information:

Calories 120, Carbs 3g, Fat 3g, Protein 18g, Potassium (K) 894 mg, Sodium (Na) 186 mg

Chili Green Beans

Prep time: 10 minutes

Cook time: 10 minutes

Servings: 2

Ingredients:

- 2 cups shredded cabbage
- 1 cup trimmed green beans
- 3 stalks chopped scallions
- 2 tbsps. chili paste
- 1 tsp. Salt
- 1 tsp. Pepper

Preparation:

1. Mix the ingredients in the Instant Pot.
2. Seal and cook on Stew for 10 minutes. Depressurize naturally.

Nutritional information:

Calories 60, Carbs 12g, Fat 0g, Protein 2g, Potassium (K) 285.3 mg, Sodium (Na) 199.1 mg

Caramelized Carrot And Onion

Prep time: 10 minutes

Cook time: 15 minutes

Servings: 2

Ingredients:

- ½ lb. chopped carrot
- 2 quartered red onions
- 3 tbsps. red wine
- 2 tbsps. butter
- 2 tbsps. herbs
- 1 tbsp. olive oil
- 1 tbsp. honey
- 1 tbsp. balsamic vinegar

Preparation:

1. Blanch the carrots in boiling water for 3 minutes.
2. Drain them, put them in your Instant Pot with butter and oil, and fry carrots, onions, and herbs on Sauté until brown.
3. Add the honey, wine, and balsamic.
4. Sauté until thick and syrupy.

Nutritional information:

Calories 129, Carbs 15g, Fat 7g, Protein 2g, Potassium (K) 378 mg, Sodium (Na) 258 mg

Roasted Parsnips

Prep time: 10 minutes.

Cook time: 25 minutes.

Servings: 2

Ingredients:

- 1 lb. parsnips
- 1 cup vegetable stock
- 2 tbsps. herbs
- 2 tbsp. olive oil

Preparation:

1. Put the parsnips in the steamer basket and add the stock into the Instant Pot.
2. Steam the parsnips in your Instant Pot for 15 minutes.
3. Depressurize and pour away the remaining stock.
4. Set to sauté and add the oil, herbs and parsnips.
5. Cook until golden and crisp.

Nutritional information:

Calories 130, Carbs 14g, Fat 6g, Protein 4g, Potassium (K) 499 mg, Sodium (Na) 13 mg

Pecan Pie Cheesecake

Prep time: 25 minutes, Cook time: 35 minutes

Servings: 10

Ingredients:

For the Crust:

- ¾ cup almond flour
- 2 tbsps. melted butter

- 2 tbsps. powdered Swerve sweetener
- ⅛ tsp. salt

For the Pecan Pie Filling:

- ¼ cup butter
- ½ cup chopped pecans
- 1 beaten egg
- ⅓ cup powdered Swerve

- 2 tbsps. heavy whipping cream
- 1 tsp. molasses
- 1 tsp. pure caramel extract
- ¼ tsp. sea salt

For the Cheesecake Filling:

- 12 oz. softened cream cheese
- 1 beaten egg
- ¼ cup heavy whipping cream

- 5 tbsps. powdered Swerve sweetener
- ½ tsp. pure vanilla extract

For the Cheesecake Topping:

- 2½ tbsps. powdered Swerve
- 2 tbsps. butter
- ½ tsp. molasses
-

- 1 tbsp. heavy whipping cream
- ½ tsp. pure caramel extract
- Whole toasted pecans

Preparation:

To make the Crust:

1. Whisk the almond flour, powdered sweetener, and salt in a medium-sized mixing bowl.
2. Stir in the melted butter until the mixture comes together.
3. Press into the bottom and halfway up the sides of a 7-inch circular spring form pan.
4. Freeze as you make the rest of the recipe.

To make the Pie Filling:

5. In a small saucepan melt the butter over low heat.
6. Add the molasses and powdered sweetener, and whisk until combined.

7. Stir in the caramel or vanilla extract and heavy whipping cream, and then stirring, add the egg. The mixture will thicken as it continues to cook over low heat.

8. Immediately remove the filling from heat and stir in the chopped pecans and salt.

9. Spread the mixture over the bottom of the frozen crust, and set aside.

To make the Cheesecake Filling:

10. Whisk together the cream cheese until softened and smooth, and then beat in the powdered sweetener.

11. Beat in the whipping cream, egg, and vanilla extract.

12. Pour this cheesecake filling over the pecan pie filling and spread to the edges of the pan.

13. To bake the Cheesecake:

14. Tightly wrap the bottom of the circular spring form pan with aluminum foil.

15. Place a large piece of kitchen paper over the top of the spring form pan, making sure it does not touch the cheesecake, and then wrap aluminum foil over the top as well.

16. Place the pan on a steam wire rack inside your Instant Pot, and pour a cup of water into the bottom of the pot.

17. Carefully lower the wrapped cake pan onto the steamer rack.

18. Close and seal the lid, making sure the pressure release valve is set to "Sealing" and then cook on the "Manual, High Pressure" setting for 30 minutes.

19. Once the baking is complete, allow for a natural pressure release.

20. Carefully remove the cheesecake and cool to room temperature, and then chill for 3-4 hours, or even overnight, before topping and serving.

To make the Topping:

21. In a small saucepan melt the butter over low heat.

22. Add the powdered sweetener and molasses and whisk until well combined.

23. Stir in the caramel or vanilla extract and heavy whipping cream.

24. Drizzle this topping over the chilled cheesecake and garnish with toasted whole pecans.

Nutritional information:

Calories 340, Carbs 4.97g, Fat 31.03 g, Protein 5.89g, Potassium (K) 204.4 mg, Sodium (Na) 252.0 mg

Molten Brownie Cups

Prep time: 5 minutes

Cook time: 10 minutes

Servings: 4

Ingredients:

- ⅔ cup sugar-free or paleo-friendly chocolate chips
- 3½ tbsps. almond flour
- ⅔ cup Swerve granular sweetener
- 6 tbsps. salted butter
- 3 beaten eggs
- 1 tsp. pure vanilla extract

Preparation:

1. Grease four 6-ounce ramekins with coconut oil spray and set aside for now.
2. Melt together sugar-free chocolate chips and butter over medium-low heat. Remove and set aside.
3. Combine the eggs, almond flour, sweetener, and vanilla extract in a medium bowl. Whisk thoroughly.
4. Pour the melted butter and chocolate into the egg and flour mixture and thoroughly whisk to combine.
5. Fill each ramekin halfway with the batter.
6. Add 1¾ cup of water to the Instant Pot and place a steamer rack into the pot.
7. Place three of the four ramekins onto the rack and stack the fourth ramekin in the center stacked on top of the other three ramekins.
8. Close and seal the lid, making sure the steam release handle in the "Sealing" position.
9. Select the "Pressure Cook" or the "Manual, High Pressure" setting and adjust to cook for 9 minutes.
10. Once done, using oven mitts turn the steam release handle to "Venting" and then do a quick pressure release.
11. Once all the steam is released, carefully open the lid and remove the ramekins.
12. Cool for 5 - 7 minutes, and then serve warm, topped with sugar-free whipped cream if you like.

Nutritional information:

Calories 425, Carbs 11g, Fat 36g, Protein 9 g, Potassium (K) 170 mg, Sodium (Na) 210 mg

Cheesecake

Prep time: 9 hrs. 10 min

Cook time: 55 min

Servings: 8

Ingredients:

For the Filling:

- 16 oz. softened cream cheese
- ¾ cup granulated Swerve sweetener
- ¼ cup heavy whipping cream
- 3 organic eggs
- Zest of 1 small lemon
- 1 tsp. fresh orange zest
- ½ tsp. pure vanilla extract

For the Topping:

- ½ cup sour cream or plain
- 2 tsp. granulated Swerve sweetener

Preparation:

1. Wrap baking parchment paper all around the sides of a 6 – 7-inch circular spring form pan. The paper should be slightly taller than the height of the pan.
2. Lightly grease the bottom of the pan.
3. Tightly wrap aluminum foil all around the bottom of the pan. Set aside the pan for now.
4. In the bowl of your stand mixer, blend the cream cheese, heavy cream, sweetener, lemon zest, orange zest, and vanilla extract until smooth.
5. Add in the eggs, one at a time, gently mixing until just combined.
6. Be careful not to over mix the eggs, or the cheesecake will be lumpy and not creamy.
7. Pour the cheesecake filling into the prepared pan.
8. Lay a kitchen paper towel over the top of the pan, and gently wrap some aluminum foil. The baking parchment paper will hold the aluminum foil in place.
9. Pour 1½ cups of water into a 6-quart Instant Pot, and place a trivet into the water with the handles facing up.
10. Close and seal the lid, making sure to set the pressure valve to "Sealing".
11. Select the "Manual, High Pressure" function and adjust to cook for 37 minutes.
12. Once the cook cycle ends, allow for a natural pressure release for 18 minutes, and then carefully open the pressure valve and remove the lid.
13. In a small mixing bowl mix together all the ingredients for the topping, and set aside for now.
14. Wearing oven mitts, carefully lift out the cheesecake and then remove the foil and kitchen paper from the top.

15. If any condensation has accumulated over the cheesecake, gently dab it off with a kitchen paper towel.
16. While the cheesecake is still warm, spread the topping over it.
17. Place aluminum foil on top the cheesecake and chill for 8 hours, or overnight.
18. Once completely cooled, gently remove the cake from the pan, also removing the outer layer of baking parchment paper, and serve cut into 8 slices.

Nutritional information:

Calories 268, Carbs 3g, Fat 23.4 g, Protein 6.8 g, Potassium (K) 28.8 mg, Sodium (Na) 239.8 mg

Pumpkin Custard

Prep time: 10 minutes

Cook time: 20 minutes

Servings: 6

Ingredients:

- 15 oz. can pumpkin puree
- ½ cup coconut milk
- ⅔ cup real maple syrup
- 1 egg
- ½ tsp. pumpkin pie spice
- Cooking oil spray

Preparation:

1. Spray a 6-inch cake pan with cooking oil spray.
2. Place a metal trivet into a 6-quart Instant Pot, along with 2 cups of water.
3. In a medium-sized mixing bowl, combine the pumpkin puree, maple syrup, coconut milk, egg, and pumpkin pie spice. Stir well.
4. Pour the pudding mixture into the cake pan and gently place the pan into the Instant Pot.
5. Lock the lid and select the 'Manual, High Pressure' button. Cook for 20 minutes.
6. Once done, let the naturally release the pressure or use the quick-release method.
7. Gently remove the cake pan from the Instant Pot.
8. Using a serving spoon, divide the pudding between six serving bowls.
9. Serve hot or at room temperature.

Nutritional information:

Calories 165, Carbs 29.9g, Fat 5g, Protein 2.2 g, Potassium (K) 305.7 mg, Sodium (Na) 22.1 mg

Chocolate Cheesecake

Prep time: 10 minutes, Cook time: 25 minutes

Servings: 8

Ingredients:

For the Crust:

- ¼ cup coconut flour
- ¼ cup almond flour
- 2½ tbsps. unsweetened cocoa powder
- 2 tbsps. butter melted
- 1½ tbsps. low-carb sweetener

For the Filling:

- ¼ cup sour cream
- ¾ cup heavy cream
- ⅓ cup unsweetened cocoa powder
- 16 oz. cream cheese, room temperature
- ½ tsp. monk fruit powder
- ½ tsp. stevia concentrated powder
- 2 large egg yolks
- 1 large egg
- 6 oz. baking chocolate melted
- 1 tsp. pure vanilla extract

Preparations:

1. Line bottom of a 7-inch spring form pan with baking parchment paper cut to fir the pan.
2. Combine all the dry crust ingredients and then stir in melted butter.
3. Using clean fingers, press the crust into the bottom of prepared pan and chill.
4. Filling:
5. Using an electric mixer blend the cream cheese, cocoa powder, and sweeteners. and cocoa powder.
6. Blend in the large egg, and then the egg yolks.
7. Add the heavy cream, sour cream, melted chocolate, and pure vanilla extract.
8. Scrape the sides of the bowl to incorporate the ingredients as needed.
9. Pour the cream cheese mixture on to the crust in the pan. Smooth the top of the filling using a rubber spatula.
10. Place a wire steamer rack in the Instant Pot, and then add in 1½ cups of water.
11. Make an aluminum foil sling and place over the steamer rack making sure the ends are long enough to extend to the top of the Instant Pot.
12. Place the cheesecake pan over the sling and cover loosely with aluminum foil to prevent any condensation from dripping on top.
13. Fold the tops of the sling loosely over the cheesecake.
14. Cover the Instant Pot and cook at 'Manual, High Pressure' for 20 minutes.
15. When the time is up, allow the pot to release the pressure naturally for 15 minutes.
16. Open the lid and gently lift the cheesecake out and set onto a cooling rack.
17. Allow to cool for 1 hour and then chill for a 2 – 3 hours before removing the side of the pan.

104

18. For the best results, the cheesecake should sit overnight in the refrigerator.
19. Serve at room temperature for a softer texture.

Nutritional information:

Calories 413, Carbs 1g, Fat 38 g, Protein 8 g, Potassium (K) 319 mg, Sodium (Na) 56 mg

Apple Crunch

Prep time: 13 minutes, Cook time: 2 minutes

Servings: 4

Ingredients:

- 3 apples
- 1 tsp. pure maple syrup
- 1 tsp. apple pie spice
- ¼ cup unsweetened apple juice
- ¼ cup low-sugar granola

Preparation:

1. In the electric pressure cooker, combine the apples, maple syrup, apple pie spice, and apple juice.
2. Close and lock the lid of the pressure cooker. Set the valve to sealing.
3. Cook on high pressure for 2 minutes.
4. When the cooking is complete, hit Cancel and quick release the pressure.
5. Once the pin drops, unlock and remove the lid.
6. Spoon the apples into 4 serving bowls and sprinkle each with 1 tablespoon of granola.

Nutritional information:

Calories 103, Carbs 26g, Fat 1g, Protein 1 g, Potassium (K) 99.2 mg, Sodium (Na) 13 mg

Spiced Pear Applesauce

Prep time: 15 minutes, Cook time: 5 minutes

Servings: 3

Ingredients:

- 2 lbs. sliced apples
- 1 lb. sliced pears
- 2 tsps. apple pie spice or cinnamon
- Pinch kosher salt
- Juice of ½ small lemon

Preparation:

1. In the electric pressure cooker, combine the apples, pears, apple pie spice, salt, lemon juice, and ¼ cup of water.
2. Close and lock the lid of the pressure cooker. Set the valve to sealing.
3. Cook on high pressure for 5 minutes.
4. When the cooking is complete, hit Cancel and let the pressure release naturally.
5. Once the pin drops, unlock and remove the lid.
6. Mash the apples and pears with a potato masher to the consistency you like.

7. Serve warm, or cool to room temperature and refrigerate.

Nutritional information:

Calories 108, Carbs 29g, Fat 1 g, Protein 1g, Potassium (K) 70 mg, Sodium (Na) 15 mg

Chai Pear-Fig Compote

Prep time: 20 minutes, Cook time: 3 minutes
Servings: 4

Ingredients:

- 1 vanilla chai tea bag
- 1 cinnamon stick
- 1 strip lemon peel
- 1½ lbs. chopped pears
- ½ cup chopped dried figs
- 2 tbsps. raisins

Preparation:

1. Pour 1 cup of water into the electric pressure cooker and hit Sauté/More. When the water comes to a boil, add the tea bag and cinnamon stick. Hit Cancel. Let the tea steep for 5 minutes, then remove and discard the tea bag.
2. Add the lemon peel, pears, figs, and raisins to the pot.
3. Close and lock the lid of the pressure cooker. Set the valve to sealing.
4. Cook on high pressure for 3 minutes.
5. When the cooking is complete, hit Cancel and quick release the pressure.
6. Once the pin drops, unlock and remove the lid.
7. Remove the lemon peel and cinnamon stick. Serve warm or cool to room temperature and refrigerate.

Nutritional information:

Calories 167, Carbs 44g, Fat 1g, Protein 2 g, Potassium (K) 464.0 mg, Sodium (Na) 4 mg

Goat Cheese–Stuffed Pears

Prep time: 6 minutes, Cook time: 2 minutes
Servings: 4

Ingredients:

- 2 oz. goat cheese
- 2 tsps. pure maple syrup
- 2 halved ripe pears
- 2 tbsps. chopped pistachios

Preparation:

1. Pour 1 cup of water into the electric pressure cooker and insert a wire rack or trivet.
2. In a small bowl, combine the goat cheese and maple syrup.
3. Spoon the goat cheese mixture into the cored pear halves. Place the pears on the rack inside the pot, cut-side up.
4. Close and lock the lid of the pressure cooker. Set the valve to sealing.
5. Cook on high pressure for 2 minutes.
6. When the cooking is complete, hit Cancel and quick release the pressure.
7. Once the pin drops, unlock and remove the lid.

8. Using tongs, carefully transfer the pears to serving plates.
9. Sprinkle with pistachios and serve immediately.

Nutritional information:

Calories 120, Carbs 17g, Fat 5g, Protein 4 g, Potassium (K) 275.2 mg, Sodium (Na) 54 mg

Chocolate Chip Banana Cake

Prep time: 15 minutes, Cook time: 25 minutes

Servings: 8

Ingredients:

- Nonstick cooking spray
- 3 ripe bananas
- ½ cup buttermilk
- 3 tbsps. honey
- 1 tsp. vanilla extract
- 2 beaten eggs
- 3 tbsps. extra-virgin olive oil
- 1½ cups whole wheat pastry flour
- ⅛ tsp. ground nutmeg
- 1 tsp. ground cinnamon
- ¼ tsp. salt
- 1 tsp. baking soda
- ⅓ cup dark chocolate chips

Preparation:

1. Spray a 7-inch Bundt pan with nonstick cooking spray.
2. In a large bowl, mash the bananas. Add the buttermilk, honey, vanilla, eggs, and olive oil, and mix well.
3. In a medium bowl, whisk together the flour, nutmeg, cinnamon, salt, and baking soda.
4. Add the flour mixture to the banana mixture and mix well. Stir in the chocolate chips. Pour the batter into the prepared Bundt pan. Cover the pan with foil.
5. Pour 1 cup of water into the electric pressure cooker. Place the pan on the wire rack and lower it into the pressure cooker.
6. Close and lock the lid of the pressure cooker. Set the valve to sealing.
7. Cook on high pressure for 25 minutes.
8. When the cooking is complete, hit Cancel and quick release the pressure.
9. Once the pin drops, unlock and remove the lid.
10. Carefully transfer the pan to a cooling rack, uncover, and let it cool for 10 minutes.
11. Invert the cake onto the rack and let it cool for about an hour.
12. Slice and serve the cake.

Nutritional information:

Calories 261, Carbs 39g, Fat 11g, Protein 6g, Potassium (K) 174 mg, Sodium (Na) 239 mg

Conclusion

Has the book given you the appropriate tools essential in eating a safe, healthy diet as a diabetic? As you can see, it is quick, simple, and delicious to eat a healthy diabetic diet!

After reading this book, it is up to you to take your health into your own hands. Adopting lifestyle and diet changes can greatly improve your condition and, in the case of type 2 diabetes, may reverse it entirely. Remember, it will take time to make lasting changes. So commit yourself to the diet and do your best to stick to it.

Diabetes can lead to some pretty devastating consequences if left untreated. For those who have diabetes, start getting it under control sooner than later. When you're ready to step up and make a change, follow the tips in this book and give some of the tasty recipes a try!

Do not let the disease control your life. Enjoy your life; remember to eat healthily and avoid smoking and heavy drinking. You can still enjoy the occasional "guilty" pleasures, but you need to restrict their consumption.

For those living with a diabetic person, I encourage you to embrace their lifestyle. It will provide them with moral support and encourage you to live a healthier lifestyle. It may even reduce your risk of developing the disease.

Appendix 1 Measurement Conversion Charts

Volume Equivalents(Liquid)

US STANDARD	US STANDARD(OUNCES)	METRIC(APPROXIMATE)
2 TABLESPOONS	1 fl.oz.	30 mL
1/4 CUP	2 fl.oz.	60 mL
1/2 CUP	4 fl.oz.	120 mL
1 CUP	8 fl.oz.	240 mL
1 1/2 CUP	12 fl.oz.	355 mL
2 CUPS OR 1 PINT	16 fl.oz.	475 mL
4 CUPS OR 1 QUART	32 fl.oz.	1 L
1 GALLON	128 fl.oz.	4 L

Volume Equivalents (DRY)

US STANDARD	METRIC (APPROXIMATE)
1/8 TEASPOON	0.5 mL
1/4 TEASPOON	1 mL
1/2 TEASPOON	2 mL
3/4 TEASPOON	4 mL
1 TEASPOON	5 mL
1 TABLESPOON	15 mL
1/4 CUP	59 mL
1/2 CUP	118 mL
3/4 CUP	177 mL
1 CUP	235 mL
2 CUPS	475 mL
3 CUPS	700 mL
4 CUPS	1 L

Weight Equivalents

US STANDARD	METRIC (APPROXIMATE)
1/2 OUNCE	15g
1 OUNCE	30g
2 OUNCE	60g
4 OUNCE	115g
8 OUNCE	225g
12 OUNCE	340g
16 OUNCES OR 1 POUND	455g

Temperatures Equivalents

FAHRENHEIT (F)	CELSIUS(C) (APPROXIMATE)
250	121
300	149
325	163
350	177
375	190
400	205
425	218
450	232

Appendix 2: Index of Recipes

Made in the USA
Monee, IL
08 November 2019